Heart

Collected Poems: 1975-2024

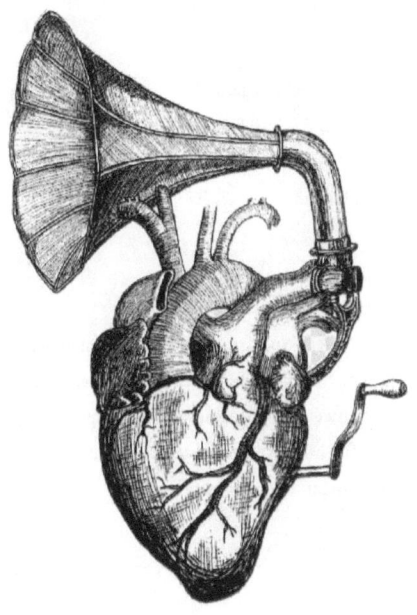

Michael Poage

Spartan
Press

Spartan Press

Kansas City, Missouri

spartanpress.com

Spartan
Press

Copyright ©Michael Poage, 2024

First Edition: 1 3 5 7 9 10 8 6 4 2

ISBN: 978-1-958182-86-4

LCCN: 2024944453

Cover image: Michael Poage

Author photos: Dr. Gretchen Eick

Acknowledgments:

First, I would like to thank Jason Ryberg, the editor and publisher at Spartan Press, Kansas City, Missouri. He has welcomed my poems, encouraged me through his own commitment to poetry, and who first proposed the idea of a COLLECTED POEMS. Also, lifelong gratitude to Shelley Hoyt and Peter Koch, Black Stone Press, who published my first two volumes of poems. I also want to thank Denise Low, Naomi Shihab Nye, Leonard Oakland, James Wright, Richard Hugo, Madeline DeFrees, Rev. R.S Thomas, Tony Barnstone, Jeanine Hathaway, William Stafford, and Luis Alberto Urrea.

I have had poems published in various journals including: *Cutbank, Chiron Review, Roanoke Review, Cumberland Poetry Review, Coal City Review, Hidden Oak, I-70 Review, Poetry Harbor, Ibbetson St. Press, Nimrod International Journal, Joyful Noise: An Anthology of American Spiritual Poetry (Autumn House), Poetry East, Pegasus, The Texas Observer, Hazmat Review, Muse & Stone, Cider Press Review, Confrontation, Chaffin Journal, Taos International Journal of Art and Poetry, Diverse Voices Quarterly, Common Ground Review, Hanging Loose, MUDFISH, River City Review, The Gasconade Review* and *CAGIBI*. I have also been recommended for a PUSHCART Prize. To the editors of these journals as well as editors of journals and magazines that are not recorded in my disorganized files, many thanks for your help along the way.

I have given readings, presented workshops, and worked in Montana, Washington, California, Tennessee, Kansas, and, overseas, in Latvia, Scotland, Bosnia and Gaza/Palestine, and the International Primary School of Mostar. I have taught at Friends University, Wichita State University, the University of Latvia, and the Medressa in Tuzla, Bosnia & Hercegovina, and, virtually, at Walailak University, Thailand. I won the Nelson Award in 2017 for the best book written in Kansas. I served as the first Poet-in-Residence at Dzemel Bijedic University, Mostar, Bosnia and Herzegovina, 2017-2018.

Table of Contents

BORN (Black Stone Press, 1975)

HANDBOOK OF ORNAMENT (Black Stone Press, 1979)

GOD WON'T OVERLOOK US
(Penthe Publishing, 2001)

ABUNDANCE (219 Press, 2004)

VOICEOVER (Blue Cedar Press, 2012)

Part I

Part II

Part III

AND SO IT GOES (POAGE, 2014)

THE COMEDIC APPLICANT (POAGE, 2015)

Part 1:   Peeling the Orange

Part 2:   Going Through Moods

Part 3: Solo

Part 4:   Shalom

THE AVERAGE LEVEL OF HAPPINESS
(Blue Cedar Press, 2016)

NOTHING A LITTLE LIGHTENING WOULDN'T FIX / 483

1.TRAVELING

2. FRANTIC

3. SILHOUETTE

AINT LEAVIN' THIS HOUSE ROUGH DRIED
(Spartan Press, 2019)

AN INCIDENT THAT MIGHT LEAD
TO SOMETHING (Spartan Press, 2020)

MIGHT

LEAD

SOMETHING

YOU MUST HAVE YOUR FAMINE
(Spartan Press, 2020)

I. WHERE ARE MY CHILDREN?

II. SCOTTISH PRAYER BOOK

III.   SCRAPE

LIES I'VE HEARD OR TOLD
(Spartan Press, 2022)

WHY THE WILL TO PUNISH?
(SPARTAN PRESS, 2023)

YOU FORGIVE, IN THEORY

THE WHOLE BRIGHT TOWN SIGHS

PHYSICAL EDUCATION

I AM USING SATIRE, OR NOT

INTRODUCTION

When you open any book of Michael Poage's poems from the last ten years, you encounter geological layers of history—layers of suffering and bloodshed, of war but also of insight and grace. And you encounter the voice of the poet--but is it his own persona or of someone he has known in Croatia, in Gaza, Bosnia—or Kansas? The need for our deep listening keeps the reader alert to the undercurrents and rip tides of these poems.

The French influenced surrealism of the early volumes is invitingly readable and often very moving to the emotional life of the mind. For example, how "Lame Deer Man" and "Alice Creek" evoke images from the years Poage spent as a sheep farmer in Montana, translating French poetry by lantern. But more than landscapes of snow, moon and dirt, we enter the charged landscapes of intimacy, of male sensuality, of the search for the lips, the hands, the glance--the search for the further depths of the beloved other as in "Breaking."

The change is notable when in his fifties the poet embraced his own sufferings (and therapy) and at the same time, due to his travels and teaching abroad, became more extroverted and aware of the suffering of those around him.

Y2K was probably not any more apocalyptic for him than it was for the rest of us, but the new millennium brought a new voice: less hermetic, more open and direct about family, travels, spiritual struggles. These don't feel like the poems of a pastor from Kansas! And yet that has been Michael's vocation, his calling: to minister to those who need, to those who don't even know how to ask. These poems are sometimes ironic in a voice that a minister cannot use in church. Some of these are weary with frustration while others whip us with a flash of bitter disappointment.

We find the poet trying to make sense of the sufferings he finds—in himself and in the war-torn world—but failing in that task he makes a poem that gives us insights and readerly satisfaction, but tragically can change nothing in the practical world.

As in any good poem, there are surprises in the last two-three lines that make us re-read and rethink our experience. He may begin with the sadness of a weeping willow but stuns us by ending: "On this date in 1812 / Beethoven wrote a passionate letter / to an unknown woman. Don't we all?" The jump to Beethoven is a surprise, but it's the final three words that give the shock.

Throughout these hundreds of poems, Poage awakens us to suffering, to jolts of acute perception, and to love at unexpected moments of grace--human and transcendent— that amazes. These wonderful short poems—they are all short flashes—reawaken in him, and thus in us, the pain of being "fully awake" in Thoreau's sense of being truly alive. And how they succeed, again and again.

-Leonard Oakland
Prof. Emeritus English Literature
Whitworth University
Spokane, WA

DEDICATION

This book is dedicated to my wife, Dr. Gretchen Cassel Eick, with all love and gratitude. Gretchen is a scholar, professor, and advisor to so many fortunate students, and a lifelong activist on behalf of justice, equality, and humanity. She has been my beloved partner in this journey of writing, teaching, and caring of family. Thank you.

Before you heal someone, ask them
if they are willing to give up the things
that make them sick.

-Hippocrates

But God bless the child that's got his own,
that's got his own.

-Holiday and Herzog

"That's enough, my darling," he said.
"You've had a cry and that'll do...
Now let's talk – we'll think of something."

-Dimitry Dmitrich Gurov to his lover,
 Anna Sergeyevna, from Chekov's,
 "The Lady with the Little Dog."
 Translated by Nicolas Pasternak Slater.
 Press, London

Writing poetry is like getting
in your ol' pickup and drivin' 5,000 miles
to a town worse than your own.

-Anonymous 14 year old
 from Wisconsin

Born

COMING APART

Something else hit my mind.
A dream
on the edge of my tongue
sweating words.

I am not alone out here
There are many of us
and tomorrow
we are moving up the road.

We have a war on our hands.
That's all I know.

REVELATION

You are in the last days
or one of them.
You are still alive,

counting the birds
as they land. The moon
is larger now than ever.

NEWS FROM BLIND GEORGE

You came across
that bridge of water
so I could see your legs.
They are gold.

I found the teeth
green as stone
swallowed to the tongue.

The arms, like flowers,
grow in the dirt.
On the elbow
an eye,
gray as rain,
covers us with sticks.

YELLOW

for Maria

Your hair is black
and quiet. On the table
a plant to eat
strangers. The glass
under the skin,
rain turns the heart
to a nest of birds.

PHOTOGRAPH

The cloth
covering the table
is stained with food.
Some old jar, scratched
and turning a new color.
We have led others here.
They often tell us
we were made for this life.
No wall could keep us in.
No cloth white enough
to make it seem like death.
Our meals are brought to us alone
and instead of flowers
there are feathers in that jar.

A HOME FOR GREEN-SKINNED LEGS

I came here
to watch you climb the rose.
The word to give life
in a time turns to me.
The man behind you
is looking for a place
to rest his eyes.
I have made you this.
It is for your legs, green
and heavy with dirt.

THE AVON CEMETERY

Mother
is the only word.
My color this year
is white
like the shirts
the men are wearing.
That storm
is here to stay.
It is getting dark
and those of us
with hats
have put them on.
You might make it
across that long
white land
but we are saved
by our own skin
and surrounded by straw.

THE FIRST PERSON WITH SKIN

The fog
she thought would cover
her bones
was only a tongue,
a door.

THE RUMOR

Nothing
more than just
a taste. Skin

like salt
and anxious
tongues work

for nothing. Come,
see my face.
Only that

one window
will open. Eyes
coming up

for air, like
reptiles, will die
to know why the dogs

are barking.

THE ORPHANAGE

That child
in the yellow cloth
has just died

of malaria. I said,
don't give me
that face again.

EDDIE FORGETS

his name.
His fish. Everyday
things.

Toast.
His orange.
The circle

of bone
he named
dog.

SWEETGRASS

Before the phone
rings
I want to write

this down.
I want
to tell you

how the snow
has turned
to rain. How

the work we did
melted white
as steel

like any man.
The wind wrapped
our faces

like cloth.
We crawled
nights

through Judith Gap,
across
the ridge, covered

our tracks
with branches,
took a bride

and showed her
someone crazy
enough.

NEGATIVELY GEOTROPIC

That means the bugs always climb higher.
They'll start at your toes
and work up
until your hair
is frosty with their sweat
and your eyes
are covered with legs.

THE POND

No obvious limb.
Windows wet
with the skin
of morning. Birds
crooked and silent
as a toad. I brush,
brush away the feathers
from your green eyes.

THE SINK

A moth in the sink.

A woman
with brown legs
touched this white edge.

I dried my skin
in the warm light
from the window.

Her hands were brown like wings.
They swam with me.

IN BED

The wind always
comes to one side
of the house. Yellow

flowers stay close
to the ground. Warm.
Safe in their weeds.

All night
that wind came
like flies through cracks

in the wall.
If it had been warmer
I would have gotten up

to kill them.

THE CHAIR

Given your eyes, mouth,
the body of your star,
you are now a window
with land behind your arms.

Your waist is cloth.
The bone is from a tree.
Your back is hard, curving
toward the open water.

THE MORNING DISTRICT

The trees are moving in the wind.
It is time for easter.
A dull star is growing in the glass.

This thing did not bleed
or bruise. The storm came down
across your face and the mountain.
You might be forgiven
even on some primitive stone.
Your body is a cave.

We hang above the river.
We count our fingers like fish below us.
There have never been flowers
like this. Your body is a cave,
it is dark
and no one even stumbles near it.

OPENING: 'moon on a box of knives'

The moon
has fingers.
The touch
comes with
light and the door
closes
with a silent
walk. The moon
walks
on it's fingers.

We wait
for a higher magic
to burn away
our arms.
Your heart
stretches
the skin
to a shadow.
We will meet
together
on your tongue.

There is never
any quiet.
At night
the bedroom

comes through
the bedroom door.
Our teeth
are made of ice.
We will be sad,
happy,
a sky with salt
for stars.

IN MY ARMS

For his birthday
a machine
to kill spiders.
I made it
with my own
hands. The years
betray him.
He whispers
in the woman-ear,
a home
for green-skinned
legs. I
am in the corner
above the door
spinning
for a saint.
Tonight
he will sleep
facing the wall.
In my arms
the breath
of a dead one
turning over
in the crawl
to find those
legs and a body
of eyes.

MY STREET

The earth was brown
and the ground was given to me.
The new moon was a shadow,
the dark face
of another round world.

I was alone in all that light,
that southern snow,
where girls cut their hair
in some room
down my street.

THE MIRROR

My face is glass.
I have not broken.
The frame around me
is the color of
my skin. I am held
to the wall by a nail.
I am not a window.
I am not your face.

WATCHING THE DOOR

It is worth it
just to have a place to sleep
and a door to close
behind me.

In this room
the only face I'll see
will fall into the river
at the end of the street.

THE SUNRISE MOTEL

When you're an old woman
you can tell your own story
but now this small room is mine
and I came here to rest,
to get away.

On the other side
of that green door
ice is broken into tiny windows
and men, younger than I am,
watch for girls going in and out.

BORN

I
In the east
there was no star.
I've mentioned this before.

There was no sun.
Leaves were burning and the smoke
made the room green.

The birds had already gone.
My breath was blood and blood.
From what I've heard
the war was nearly over.

II
That was the end
of my fat woman period.
I was born in Peru.
No. No.
In the south,
in this country.
Near dinner time.

III

A simple ceremony
like breaking a mirror.
A crazy green turtle
fought his way past
the guards to tell me
I was his father. As a child
you remember
those things. The feel
of his shell is still
with me. The glaring love
in his eyes
makes me wonder
if he wasn't right.

IV

There are birds
with blue feet.
Someone tell us
if the door opens,
our noise may carry
through these walls.
We've been kicked
out of places before.
You may have seen us
running from my father.
There was light,
warm as skin,
on the window.

V

My body is too big
for my head.
I walk in the shadow near the wall.

The street shines in the rain.
The sun is blowing
and drifting
across our land.

We vanish
like wings into trees.
My head is too big
for my body.

VI

"You were sold for nothing, and you
shall be redeemed without money."

I am early.
Old men call this winter open.

I've worked in blood
all my life. Now, follow me
to my own door.

Come and drink the bride.

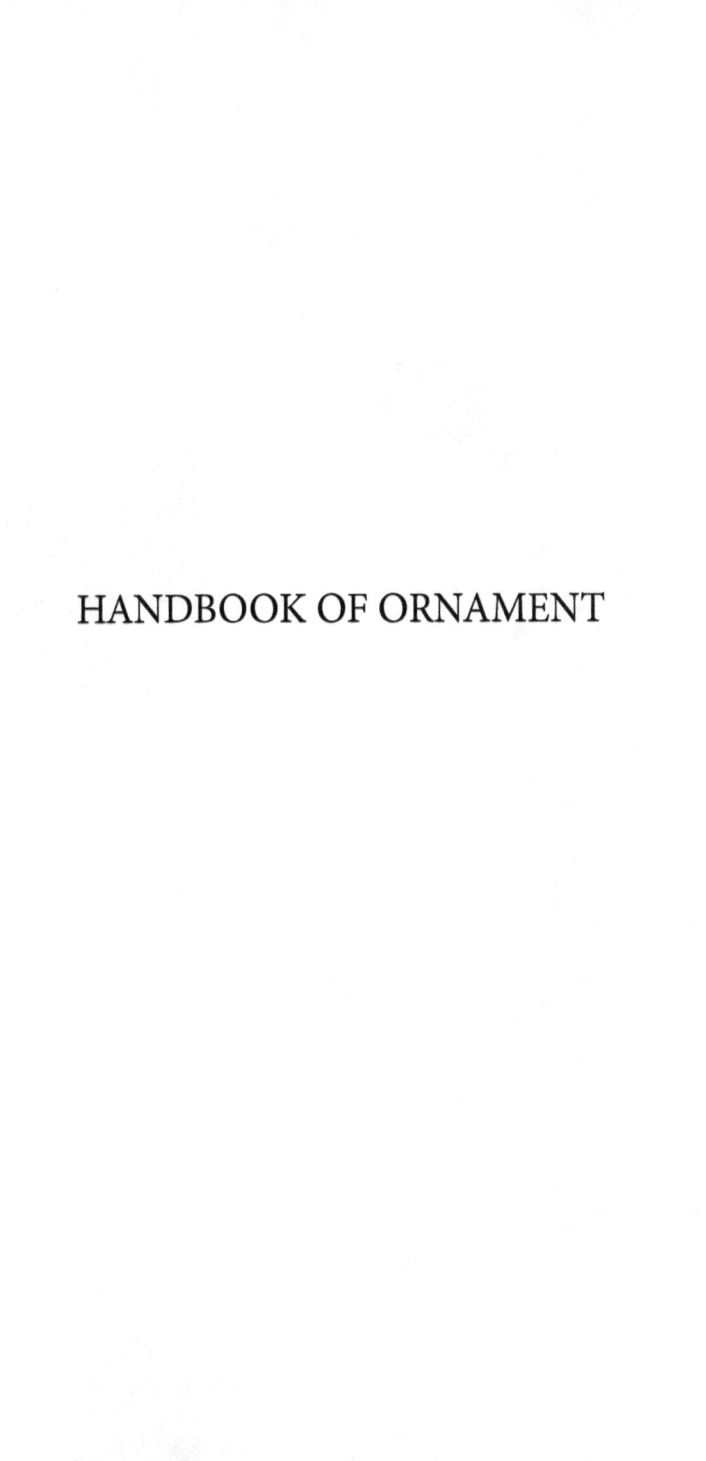

HANDBOOK OF ORNAMENT

LAUREL

Down to words
and very little else.
The night
is soothing every
mouth.

On the edge
of laurel eyes,
crowns of laughter
and sleep,
your warm knees
hold the ground
like roots.

The lather
of your breathing
soaks the air.

OPENING:

'And when he came up out of the water'

While I've been gone
I've seen birds,
blind fish,
ants making hands
on the pavement.
Many of you
were there.
During the night,
the words burned
a light-year away
with names meant to be hidden
like the heart.

Blood flew
on wings of hair.
The good-luck bird
watched newborn eyes
beneath the skin.
Out of the garden
you are someone else
and your lips glow
like an orange star

That hand is mine.
I watch my white hair
like a field and near the bed
the house is yellow.

I'm sure of that color.
Please don't crowd
the doorway.
From the stomach
of this room
I will go to other towns,
none of you are there.

THE WINDOW

In my chair on this side
of the window I am warm.
I can see in this room
from one wall to the door.
On the other side
snow dull as earth.
in her blue robe my wife
passed through that pane.
On the other side
snow dull as earth.

YES

It hangs
like a souvenir

of the night.
No more

walking into caves
with my mouth

round as an egg
and the baby

crawling across
my tongue. Animals

living here
have tracks you'll never see

until it's dark.
They come as bites

on your skin
and as night.

They come to us
in clay boats

from surviving
stars. The girl

named for a mountain
has turned to snow.

She falls like light
on her bed

and I bury my eyes
in the roots of her hair.

REQUIEM

Old men
married to their skins
return to black
oceans and wait
like daughters for dawn.

Everything sleeps
except the drifting tears,
waves, the shallow kisses
of earth. Who will dress the shore
with white trees
and birds? Star after star
dying from death to darkness
erases itself
from the sky.

The doors, the hands,
the subways of noon
shower down on us
like mountains. We dive
across the soft map,
the desert we love.
The leather of whales, the flame
from inside the brain,
and the arms come like lightning
to embrace our lap.

They wrapped her
in green cloth
like a tongue floating in the grass.
It is not a love of words.
We came from swamps, settled the land
with our new arms, flesh
like snake and eyes like fish
swimming coastal shadows.
We have died in beds of rivers.

THE BEGGAR

Rumors of mice
and small birds
fill the air.
Most of us
are lost,
stink of snow.

At noon,
in the moonlight,
trees burn
their skin.
It has quieted down
to rain
and snow in the higher
mountains. My brother
digs graves
in this mud.
I have my own life.

JUNE

I was wrong.

Winter bones, given up
for dead,
circled the night.
My old-woman anger
could kill the quiet.

Now there is nothing
to hide my face,
my dark wall.

LAME DEER MAN

The last word
will stop you.
I am going
the other way,
through country
made for sheep
or dying dogs.
That's all.

Even in the dark,
the heat of day,
ten years are gone.
Heads down.
A prayer
to heal the lame
or bring down the wall.

Blood flows
like a river
in the skin.
The winter
ran it to the ground.
The children dream
a yellow moon.
They shout from their room,
their lives
have all gone hungry.

A NEST OF BIRDS

I am black.
The nest is gold.

I shine
like a starling.

Catching my breath,
I watch women

cutting through my hedge.
My sleep is scattered

like people in the street.
The crooked love

you feel in your veins
is a blue wall

with three eyes.
I hear your teeth

turning flesh
into oceans of ice.

A needle of light
lies down in that quilted room

and like a snake
it's more afraid of you.

OPENING:

'And each wound has the shape of your mouth'

-Neruda

The fog
comes to us
like a shell.
We move
within the grey flesh,
wet and hard
as the eyes of a machine.

We move like the earth
under your blouse.
You touch my glass foot
and the breeze
lifts your skirt
like a wave.

I swim toward the warm bread
of your legs
breathing below the water
and stretching across the table
I ask for your mouth
with my mouth.

SOMATIC:

'shocked by a flower, dismembered by a kiss'

-Dupin

The outer walls
of the body
are disguised.

The soul is discovered
in a coat of wire
woven in the pattern

of the earth.
'Your lips

are like scarlet thread'
Your kiss
comes like a garden

blue as water.
My heart is a cradle,
a flute,
and the song
carries your name
across the blind river.

WATER

A dark tide
carried eyes
down. Like a bird
in the green light

you searched the sea
for food. We've seen
your poison
stun a fish

for hours,
hold him for a meal.

Your appetite
huddles with us
here in the corner.

We will have our rags,
each other,
to eat.
You pushed my arms,
your skirt,
away.

THE MOST DISTANT EPOCH

Before our time
we sat in boats of snow
drifting toward light.

Before fire
we slept in grass

and listened
for animals
eating our words.

THE BRIDE

There are bricks
in the air.
I catch
my breath
and hold it
like a man.

Lions,
you said,
would meet me
at the door.

I've never seen
your face,
my eyes.

THE HISTORY OF HAIR

Daylight is more
than I asked for.

The ground
covered us
like cold sleep
falling around
our ears.

EDDIE'S DREAM

As a child
I hated tonight.
Feeding under the table
I buried my lips
close around
your heart.
The mirror
moved over my skin
like a body of air.
The street,
a dark leg
squirming like night.
My gift for you,
a bed coming alive.

A FLIGHT OF BIRDS

Your hair shines
like a street.
The bridge is falling

from your heart
and you carry yourself
like a candle

filling the air
with blackbirds
and their red wings.

LOVE

The road leaves us
here. The first blood
comes from where I
breathe. Alone
in the grass
I have one face.
The old man
gone like an atom.
I write letters
and drop them between the T.V.
and the wall.
This world
is for my father,
husband, whose bones
clutter the roof
of my mouth.

'Such is death, with her daring husband'
                              -Vallejo

Over near the sun
the legs of leaves walk
across the room.
Against all odds
I saw her, arms of hair,
and the lost house
of her insect shade.
She moved around the table
whispering like a bird,
the sky a molecule of sleep.

OPENING: Repairing the Fence

The snow
is sticking to our eyes.
Stones
the size of hail
cover our clothes.
We live in the walls
and love the darkness
between the sheets.
The earth
listens to our feet.
Our blue fur
hangs from the fence
like fingers
and my hands
bleed like wire.

LISTENING

There are walls
in these ears.

Again in the night
the wise and the warm
are names.
Never.
Nevermore.

The endless covering
of gentle blood.
Dame. Countess. Gentle
and blue.

DYING OF COLD

Your knuckles
and hands

are white
from all the water.

We move
to many cities

taking each other's
life. Swaying

like planets,
tasting each other's

life, we travel
the backbone,

whisper
the one word

warm enough
for any frozen lips.

WORDS

The fire
looks like water
to your eyes.

Your eyes
fall like hair
on this paper.

'The moon at last undresses'
                    -A. Bosquet

She opens the window
and the mountains
are the faces of men
with cloudless eyes
skin swelling like sand
and mouths open
to catch the snow.

THE WORLD BODY: Fiber

Bliss followed you
from the east. I see

in your veins
the blue waters

and the glow
of a hollow

eye. Your heart,
a bowl of fat

clothed in grass.
We breathe

a sky of hair,
a larva ghost

wrapping the tears,
the trees,

in solitary
silk.

ALICE CREEK

The light steps through
rain. Needles or sharp teeth
point to other trees,
branches of living air
lacing the birds
with black water.

the arm with twelve wives

eyes light
the morning skin
that holds my face
together
arms in the air
that moon is no lady
on the inside your fathers
take you back I smell
my way to the room
the windows are black
because the sun
is black the mirrors
show all of you
the way home we watch
the world
through slits in the wall
we start from nothing
fragments of living
matter a single cell
divided in silence

AGAIN

When you open me up
stay close
to the glands. Below
you will find
hair standing
on end. Orange
throats make it
easy to breathe. Wives
always careful
that is what I mean.
Yes. We meet
only in secret,
in the darkness
of firing-squad
red brick.

THE NEW TRIBE

That face
not to be given again.
That mirror
of broken glass
speaks a language
seldom heard today.

The river
is still home.
Coming in above the trees
we keep an eye
for signs of life,
that face.

HANDBOOK OF ORNAMENT

I
You can see
the yellow
of her face,
the poison
of a lion.

Her hair
sprayed with darkness,
the fingers of ladies,
earrings,
last love coming fire.

II
Hungry to eat
halos,
those glowing throats

are jewels
around black necks.

III
To your left
you see the tiny village
etched above angel lips.

The planets will cry.
The lips of the pelican
will skim the salt
like the breaking of a heart.

IV
My own hands changed
when my son
turned six.

The flesh was covered
with words. Glancing above you,
see how the legs
cover the village.

The rugs,
woven by fallen women,
are Portugese.

V
On 'this shore made of lips'
we are all
asleep
with the leopard,
her mouth,
water,
water.

THE GOSPEL OF MARY

BEDTIME

The baby is asleep
upstairs. I have one hour
to breathe
in my own
radiating beauty,
in the blue mist
of the mirror.

Downstream
to a deadlock,
fresh water falls
on my child's hand,
goodnight
and the moon.
The sky is as old
as she is.

MOTHER'S ISLAND

My red hands
color the body
like a fish in a palace.
In a flame of braids
I bring the boat home
like a sweet sailor
to his wife.

This captain
is made to be sad.
On the wall
islands not for navigation
or a man
in the ivory air.
I would like to eat
like a toy, a round body
to cut through
and turn over.

This ancient site
dwarfed by turtle grass,
anchored in the brown
and black, survives
like a crab, female
figures I have seen.

From this subtle pouch
as many die
as are born.
A pocket for a heart,
water for the blunt and blue.
It is a feast
under the arm
of the curator,
portrait of a man
owned by private hands.

I would like to eat like a toy.
On the face of it
tender-eyed
an ocean
on the orchard floor.

In this light
I am a walking rose
in the ear of winter,
past the sun,
past mournful women,
a popular drink.

THE BLUE COAT

I miss the river
going to darkness,
the diseased stones
of shame.
       I throw the unclean
outside the city   bathe the walls,
the bed
with lament.

The sickness of the cloth
must mourn the brave
and swallow
       the bargain song.

This is the law
for a language
with no future. My throat
is waiting for the next ice,
one gentle night
unused except by grass.

I carry an illegal name
       grab my heart
with deeds for burial.
I have some desire
for advantage, to lie
       between the paralyzed
and the odd savior.

AFTER PRAYERS

It's time to go
outside and get the paper.
It is still dark
but good or bad
the words and pictures
never seem to care/

I call early in the day.
You reach the phone
just in time. Always
missing someone, you say.
I say, yes.

STORMBOUND

Swimming at the sea
I'll guess how to move
toward you. The paper snow
was no winter at all.

That first memory
was the end of the world
like the air today.

NORTH BEACH

What happens now
in the salted rain?
We need winter, some cold
and perfect night.

But back at the house
with the walls dying
and the hollow doors
like bloodless neighbors

we watched the slow opening
of a fat dawn.
No swimming here.
Tide too strong.

The stomach dropped
to its knees.
These are tears.
That's how this sea works.

THE CONFUSION RANGE

The part of his body
he needs most
is night.
How can you stand this?
Driving south past groves
of orange and lemon,
past fields of cotton,
it was the best time
in years, maybe ever.
See this portable man
with many lies on his lips,
his face falling
closer to the ground.

I need to stay nearby.

Soon, the bodies found
will make convincing evidence.
The booming sport
of disintegration will have no reward.
The dead are kind.

I've tried dancing
but I make moves
against my will.
These mountains make it worse.
The trees are bled empty,

pale as stone.
The birds come to us
but the stars
have another desire.
Every lake is edged with ice.
Confused as I am
I must stay nearby.

OPENING: "Has the rain a father?"

As for me
the blur of speech
or sleep
makes the rain
a hard steal.
It makes the father
imperative
in a language
of bad money,
blackmail
in the smallest town.

A sad pocket
moves with the leg.
If I were feeling
any better
I'd be a runaway.
My quiet voice
doesn't carry
past the table.

When you go leave no trace,
no profile.
The complexion
of your shadow
will glow in my hand
like the blindness

of snow, the mole-eyed witness
to another sea
of land, veined and bridled,
an orange flame
to any eye
dead but moving
with the leg.

PRIESTLY HOUSES

The story of Jericho is not clear.
Our remains
are inferior to those
found near us. Our language
is now a foreign dialect
forcing a southern smile.
The mouth of the cloth
committed to begging,
a mendicant order
when the sea lays down.

I take what I can
in my hands, dissolve
a new style, too much
in this landscape and a fear
that may never again open us up.
Never leave me. I am the queen
of refuge, the sugar and the flesh
from paradise to the wrong memory.

Where I live
sleep is a mirage,
a light burning in the window,
companion for an empty sky.
Down the back flow the tears
you will never see.
Crazy. In the white that follows
from boyhood on
I know this is the birthplace of someone.

MADONNA OF THE ROSE-TRELLIS

In the many shades of red
the grass drawing new color,
the smell of anatomy, the sound
of secondary questions
pounding like righteous rain.

No mother alive
in the many shades of red,
bright as a bowl,
a new conception holding a stick
above the silent child.

Now the tears we forgot
in the mountains of our hands
in the many shades of red
make a wave of storm-cries
and mud and shoes.

Your eyes are blossoms in a tree.
The animal surrounds us now
and speaks in the secret ear.
In the many shades of red
our memory a victim of fire.

Yesterday, at this time,
we lived there fifty years,
a crawl space in the sheer sky,
your breathing woven to a smile
in the many shades of red.

BLIND GUIDES

I am ironing
the last wrinkles
from my wedding dress.
Though the blue
is color-blind
the debris
of occupation
stands like a city,
an irregular surface
from the age of iron,
older than human memory
or the cap of death.

This is the last chance
for a holy land tour.
All the rivers
had babies
but me. It is not mourning
when you say,
"If I had not known you,
I would not have found you."

Judah Street
appears first
as oppression
but is born
into a further light.

In the southern quarter
of the sky, cold hands
broken like a field.
This goddess
escapes every dress.

SERENADE

I listen to a parade
on the radio. Figures of fun
as in all dreams
you had made your own.
Birds, photograph of a corner,
your house broken down
by the roof of the world,
a face between the knees.

The pale rocks,
the shrinking of the lake.
No peace is easy. We are clear
of snow and love.
The paper spits a name
through the window air.

A woman came into the floor.
She was empty
and speaking through a river
of nails. Under the clouds
clear-bodied men
surround our table, a thread of flesh
like a finger. After dinner
our legs fold up under us.
Tell me what survived
and what did not.
I still see black.

Your time is always ready.
You see your body
as something
you can heal,
bits of cloth
carried from a burning home.
In these days of suspicion
we are eyed
like a blue bargain
of leaves and limbs
full bloom and welcome
kissing each face
like a magnet.

THE ROOM

Each wall
is closed
and I am left
alone. That white door

is the color of your face.
It is hot
along every river

here in the east.
Our skin
rubs off like dirt

and I must stay here
and watch you.

THE OLD CITY

Taking care
not to paint the grass
the wrong color
I follow instructions
to the letter. My health
is a storm
with lightning
and thunder above the snow.
I see my breath
in the air. I hear the fire.
This morning

what good
does warm air do?
The heart is fighting
all the rules, my stomach
on the edge of screaming.
We are free of crime
but I have a trembling kiss,
my deliverance
to any green pasture,
to any wall that weeps.

THE DROWNING

Against isolation,
holy week
and whether this man inside,
with the sea so close,
can watch the only tree
through the only window.

How can we explain it?
When did it get started?
The sky was a white horse
with another door
open to fear and deformity.
There are no survivors
in these stories.

A hotbed of mare
and the lame, nights
made short. We rescued two
from an empty sea.
Never forget me
or my real appearance,
my last words.

I hear
there's a gospel of Mary.
It is a fragment
and she is naturally saddened.

A NEW BODY IN THIRTY DAYS

Even in this small room
you see treasures. The light
of no one's body
falling away like the sky
above a farm.
The anger of the lake
is good and evil
sharing the man
sad in your eye.

Now, you form the life
of the family. In this model
for the origin of breathing
we need a neutral shade.
That clarifies the sacrament,
slapping the face
of the lonely lake
sad in your eye.

The dead hands,
the voice of classic neglect,
snow turned to glass
for everyone to be happy.
Nothing wrong with being tough
in a frozen light,
your next of kin,
redeemer
sad in your eye.

BREAKING

How many people am I?
All the prior claims
against this scalding winter
are valuable common ground,
just ask those involved.

The words we use
to make light in love,
to shrink a temporarily enlarged
heart, fill our lives
with human poems.

In this scattered night
shining in the ground
like the pasture grass
and the rain I fall this morning
from her intimate lamp.

The birds are flying like geese
over a beach unsafe
for swimming. The arms of my watch
open to take me in.
How many people am I?

DRIVING TO WORK

I saw the sun
this morning—
how it moved across the face
of traffic,
into the city
waiting out the dark.

In today's paper
a plastic heart
failed to get a man
on his feet.
I am a storm
you said last night
and I am full of rain.

For almost forty years
I've stayed away.
I could touch
only the bad weather.
The wedded lightning
kissed me
and it was a familiar
injury.

CONTRIBUTIONS

for Sarah

I will give you
this saddle
for your mirror. The beauty
is slow to smile
and all the color
is gone. In your room
I saw a pillow
shaped like a horse. The dust
swims in my eyes.

My love for you is here.
Now that all the things we say
are sad and good
your voice
will grow across the moon
without me.

We all remember
someone else. Give whatever you can.
One more thing. We are each other.
The rain beats against your heart
and mine.

ANGEL ISLAND

*"Nor were those the waters
of the heart she heard"* (P. Levine)

There was no talk
of tomorrow. Remember the human
door, swarms
keeping the shopgirls
all the rage. I should be
into clothes gathering dust
since before you knew me,
tears shining like birth,
a few days in the year
drinking only daylight.

But the danger is the smile
of anger in thin air.
On slopes of sky
our faces are weak,
another storm
to wash away our land.
My memory aches
for some picture of that love,
an inside light
taking time but healing.

FARM

Your neck, more stone
than skin. A birthday
with many candles
and a breath as dark
as the ground.

Plowing early this year
waking up to storm
the family nerves,
poor words for love
and work.

Coffee and large plates
on a silent table.
The curtains
covering the window
are almost white.

MEADOWLAND

The water is moving
with no river
to carry it. Bring me
another view,
a distant empire
with many faces,
ancient violations,
souvenirs
glittering in the window.

Her hair was matted
with colored clay.
We translate
the right word
for dying, dying.
Tears are not new.
Smiling as ever
she rubs her eyes
against the wood.

Normally exhausted
she is warm and red
in a false ceremony.
Her country of love
is a cloud
abandoned by the sky
and her eyes are swift
to own her loss.

The baby is talking now.

Her skin burns
in the sun. Cleaning
house, she smokes
and drives the dust
to one corner.
She has a new waist
but cries for arms
of slender peace.
It has rained every day.

She runs the other way.
The crowd gathers
to help
themselves. They use
their native language.
The street is moving,
killing her river,
burying even tears.
Why kiss only sadness?

OPENING: "oil to make his face shine"

Below the frail
words of the air,
the wet ground
poured its neck of land
into another wave,
the opening of a hand.

Those nights
the children cry,
streams of darkness
paint the wall
a tidal color, block the doors
with famine, the windows with thirst.

The first line
of fraud, the city street
with birds like dimes
natural as trees,
that was his full face.
Wind-fall
clear to the river,
throat touching throat, his shirt
scattered cell by cell
down the canyon of roses
wild and locked
in shrouds of song.

This is the marriage
of fallen stories.
A letter from the prison
came with this kind
of music.

INELEGANCE

White-washed
and skin
deep,
how sure am I?

Heart and I
stand in the open air
exterior like a net
crazy eyes
at the turn of the tide.

PLANS FOR COAL MINE, REVIVED

It was mentioned
in the news
in place of his dying father
as the sky opened
and the pride of stars
invented bitter weather
and words I cannot finish.

Grass on a hillside
and the taste of stones
turned over
bring a promise of new life
and new death.

They say this climate
will prosper
and we'll all be richer
from the years. They say this picture
gives a good idea
of life in the mine.
Our deformity is passed on.
Our fear is fed with rhyme.

RODEO

Thirty Vigils
in this town.
Also Bliss Mahan.
There is instant weather
and old is welcome.
I'm no morning star.
I don't believe
in holy cities.

From the window
there is nothing
but the ash-blond
as queen
in her blue dress.
All the intimate
and pale strangers
bring the east wind
and rain.

My daughter
points to the sky,
to the tender red
on the black clouds.

PRAIRIE

I wrote these
before you could talk.
Clear nights
were gone
and the fading hills
like my arms
were brown.

Out of earshot
pearls drummed the neck
whispered in the trees
how the stone's face
deep-mouthed and hollow
shook the dead
and the frozen air.

Nothing
as a husband.
Then there was rain
like a curtain,
west to east.
Dark farms
abandoned,
wind still turning
water.

PORTRAIT OF THE EARTH

I pictured myself living
at all ends
of the earth. I mean well,

wear my heart
on the edge.
I regret

the usual color,
the red shale
of the floor. The fault

or dashed lines
from my eyes
to the curve

of these scattered layers.
What do I do
to make this map?

Observe the ledges
or artificial jumps,
the strike of beds.

We follow the symbols,
patterns redrawn
and completely stripped away.

IMAGINARY HUMAN

Things aren't the same.
My hands again
focused on the fire
in the snow. The houses

are blind. Old walls
of failed stone
overwhelm our surprise,
it's a giant

at eye level.
I brought an edible circus
for the bright eyes.
I rode

a thinking cloud
in Texas. But now I don't live
that way. A blouse
of triumph

and jars of food
for my pain. The siren
stops nearby. I am taken
from my home. My picture

is news, a lonely
white cow

between cannibals
and cardinals. Yes

and in our elegance
we kiss the drawled mouth.
Our flow of words
is deaf to silence.

Point-blank and labored,
our tongue is denied
and in the end
the giant dies.

THE BLOOD OF CHRIST MOUNTAINS

Somebody told us
a certain place
where the new harvest
posed as a future flower,
a cold guilt
caught red-handed
in fresh grain.

Gardens lie
in the heart of the city.
Our own taste
now made sacred
in the snow. And later,
with hands like ravens
and eyes older
than the earth,
you shouted a dream
with no waking,
no sleep.

In these last weeks of the year
lamentation is a portrait,
someone saying,
go to Jerusalem,
the beauty is there.
But I was never young
enough to sweep it

off my feet. We moved
between familiar lives,
against the escape
or entry of air. And with our
compound eye
we see this drop of water
as a circular field.

Breathing stopped three times.
They all crowd the shore
quoting prices, assuming names.
Small holes in the fabric
permit a view of the world.

The morning clouds
grow white, then black
for an early storm.
Fields of yellow grass
and skirts in the river
bend to the dark rain.

NO MISTAKE

How many lives
does it take? Lovers who stand together
know. Those who fall apart know
something else.
             We've seen so many photographs
of children – Whose are these?—
paintings of barns and birds,
the house of a widow
with time now for light
and a new cloud.
             I've read new words
on sin, seen a new movie on the birth of
Christ,
heard the good and the bad of living
in Jerusalem.
             Now I hear a tender
trumpet. If these are the last days
I don't want to know. If these hands
can do nice things, our gift spreads
             like a cloth. Before its goodbye,
the grief comes gray as wanting.

SWEEPSTAKES

I
We finished our game
of identifying birds.
We heard the call

of strange flight
begging out loud
our intentional disease.

We wear the land
like sad cloth
crippled from birth.

II
Her father went back
to another wife. The scars
of course are open

and a small pain
covers the eyes, no song
of songs

would win this heart.
I toured the wrong country
with a knife

and my white blood
was a sure sign
of terror.

III
Constant talk
on the radio, a doctor
counseling death,

music without words.
Here is a land
with no sky to open.

PELAGIC

In the breath
of a hand
we saw a small bird
swimming in the air.
We returned
to home's street.
The moon
is a human back
caught again
in an act of passion
and condemned
with all its beauty
and common questions
to the open sea.

READY FOR THE SEA

I swallow with my hands
trying out a blossom
for taste. Speak of glowing
and cradling, some remain
close to your side. The light
surrounds your eyes
with a little love,
a blue knife
and almost nothing. A touch
of weather brings this desert
to life, a shadow of pleasure
like a thorn in the white grass.
You open the envelope bomb,
a wasp in clay, blond hair
in the hands. The pain
of running water
and the sprawling winds
close your eyes. No gold veins
in modern times. Every known map
buried in the air.

MAIDEN VOYAGE

It's me again.
I've never been
on my own like this
and it's strange. All this time
alone. I could read
or take a bath.
Call anyone.

Where will I eat tonight?
Who will see me
reading my map?
When I go home
I will take off my shoes
and warm my feet on the heater.
I will watch the window.

If I could open my hands
to someone in this sea
some brief light
could empty my belief.
A glance into a face,
one cup on a table,
a long letter.

What am I? I am a kid
with a memory for endings.

"I FIND SOME STARS THAT I
BELIEVE IN HANG THERE DEAD"

-Sandra McPherson

Each domestic murder
adds a new word to the river,
a bloodless laugh, another goodbye
from the earth, from a star
we thought alive.
        I speak
to every neighbor, bring the desert warmth
into winter homes. I wish them health
and happy thoughts. I mention
my daydream last night, how aggressive
with territory I was.
        We sat down
by the streams of Babylon and wept.
Now open your Bible
and read it several times. Give it a new name
using frantic. The bruise
grows out of pity
for surrounding tissue. The distant children,
rerouted by storms, ice on the runway,
read my letters and I kiss the pages
blue and black.

RUMORS OF SUNDAY

Once off the cross
and birth
is out, still below
the knife, I remember
the color of the sky
and the military
kiss. My appetite
married to the waves
rolling down your face
to the fortified
memory of a phone-call
and a whisper
tapping on the lungs.

Forgiveness was photographed
weeping on the porch
forever. Someday
I'll write
a real letter
while the trees outside
share a shattered
horizon. Silent singing, the baby
learning wall, dirt and snow
at a smooth angle
like a torn lip.
My black sweater
surprised you.

SEMI-PRECIOUS

Terminal is not a word.
On a Sunday afternoon
the outer body – a daughter –
is born a dead lake
in a weaponed winter.

I see green clouds
shaped by the wind
the way you look at me
as you escape on paper
wings into another room.

MANHUNT

Sweet lilac
and the snow
are habits we lost.

Red Earth
murdered a wife.
And the river is gone,

and the house.
After this story,
life is nothing.

It is not a good time of year,
rebuilding a face
from memory.

MARILYN RECAPTURED

Red line on a wing,
a surviving light
speaking from the waist
and the empty
eyes like an argument
from silence. Only words
crawl from the opening
and the gracious bomb,
the please run away,
no wing to pull now,
red line my hand.

DECEPTION ISLAND

There are black cows
and red ones. This far
east of the mountains
the blizzard moves
from grief to storm.

I noticed the swans
paired and gliding from the shade
to the blood-water of Europe.
But it wasn't Europe.
Some other backyard.

The disabled man
across the fence
spoke an odd language,
easy to make fun.

Stillborn
with hands to count
the good stories
but fighting fifty years
of lost ground. He said –
I gave myself children
and begged them
not to grow.

MAPMAKER

Breaking the father-face
use care, strangle
the air. I write
like a child, my letters
make no sense. I am lost
               in punishment.

You can cry
about another home,
small things
that breathe. A summer
of strange locations,
running the risk
of never finding help.

Sweet and not sweet.
I like secrets.
Dislike openness.
Don't let the phone ring.
Mapmaker, hear me,
say ...
dry lake, unimproved
road.

A SONG

The lake is empty.
From the top of my heart
I thank these mornings in the sun.
I say hello to you
and hope you hear me.
Remember, remember,
who holds you.

From the top of my heart
all that is hurt
catches the wind with a new face,
new eyes at each glance.
After talking with one so desperate today
my own dark time speaks softly,
other tears warm the room.

I've never felt so full,
so stuffed with war.
I study the landscape and hope
the snow is right. I am already missing the truth,
yet I have just found it.
I breathe the air that comes in blessings
and unfold letters wrapped in fire.

The birds on the road this morning
raged into my lungs. Their feathers
left me dying, safe, named.

'It's a small day tomorrow.'
Remember, remember
who holds you.
The lake is empty.

291

At the Whitney
we hear this quote:
"Darkness is another name
for light...."

At the apartment
we leave the windows
open slightly
all night.

I am 45 now
three weeks after
we caught the cab
to Penn Station
and remembered the white walls
and hair of Stieglitz,
and a long, dark
light kiss.

THE SPREADING PONDS OF SATICOY

The lyric is gone here.
The water old.
Any sadness has turned
to poker-faced prayers.

Take the junked cars,
table-scraps,
your tired look,
for instance.
Such a thin face
sharp as razored words
on lace.

Like a ghost
standing in the distance
the sour taste
remains on your lips.
You melt with that kind
of affection.

COUNTRY MUSIC

Kansas is a river.
Grass and cottonwood,
secret homes and graveyards.
It twists and turns
in shallow sleep
awake to a wide hour
of dust and love.

AS THE BRIDEGROOM REJOICES IN THE BRIDE
SO YOUR GOD WILL REJOICE IN YOU

After breakfast
they go back to bed.
The phone does not ring

and the last sonnet
to Orpheus speaks
the I am and then closes

the darkness like a lover
turning to leave. Simple
sensual dust

dance with me,
male or female.
The ground is moving

and my hair is soft and gray.
Now the traffic outside
is moving too,

O gentle God,
making love
into something else.

FOUR-MILE CEMETERY

Some
say that in heaven
everyone wears pink.

What Laura saw
faded in and out
from grey
to barely grey.
Her mother had a Bible
verse for every occasion.
Even for a child bleeding.

They talk as if
the light went out
in her eyes.
I must lead them
to the grave.

There are the footsteps
of my neighbor
out in the hallway
that separates her west side
from my east.
Her door shuts hard.

Out in the field
beyond the leaning stones

and fallen strands of wire
cattle of all colors
move toward the water
together.

ASH WEDNESDAY

Not speaking for the other
yet the words are shared
beneath the burning waves
repeating the confession of light
across the breast and arms,
now the face. Strings for adagio,
a moon always appearing
within the believable sky.
A black cross on their hands, ashes
from a Kansas bowl my grandmother
used for jello. Now the words move
toward the cross on the ceiling
above the ten of us standing
in the light/dark of sanctuary.

HEART AIRPORT

Departure leaves the runway
gray and black
as another plane
dreams life
into more.

Swinging into sunlight
makes me younger
bringing a smile
along the rain-eyes
bright and hollow.

Leveling off at a speed
we never feel until descent
you are always moving,
always older, touching down
with skill and sorrow.

BE MINE

She pointed out the crocus
last night breaking into open air.
Then mentioned the danger
of the next few days.
No smile rested her face.
"The cold will come hard
on Valentine's Day."
I need to go on,
to break a window,
to face myself, my child.
This begins another spring
of God only.

FUNERAL

Kansas, 1985

Yesterday, as I put the ashes
in the ground, the gravedigger's
hat blew away. Somewhere
between the stones
he grabbed it.

Such a sacred time
not because it is holy
but so human.
The family stood like stalks
of corn with tears.

Into the empty air
I made some words
go cold, asked God
for a face of light
and arms to hold

grief, this harvest,
until we're done
and our breath
runs the cattle
home.

LAMBING TIME

You feel more like a husband tonight,
more domestic, homespun. The animals
are fed and you sit on the edge of the bed
quiet and think of the kids, getting them
to school in the morning, caring for the lambs,
writing in the afternoon. On the edge of things
now though, thinking the past is the present,
but knowing that is not working. The arctic
air is coming to end the warmest January
on record. Singing into the air on the silent
porch filled with sunlight, the first Imagist
poem doesn't come to mind, nor does the last.
Spring is suicide time. Statistics. What do they know?
I just barely keep my eyes open while you
struggle to get your wool pants on over jeans,
your red suspenders over shoulders, and holding a flashlight
to find the babies dropped in the dark
snow. Day changed to night so quickly.
It takes my breath away. I heard that song on the radio
today. There is music all around us but I just don't believe
the words.

OPENING: *'Miss Graham leaves no immediate survivors'*
(The New York Times)

We dance this circle
that twists
like a spring. We are all

immediate survivors.
Our steps
each a lonely hope

moving away.
The enemy
is leaving home

at 45. To be happy
is to break
a lifetime.

THE WEDDING

The sky
was like a face
radiant

and cloudy.
The breeze
filled a tree

with small birds
disturbed.
The bride waited

thinking her children
would give her
away.

SAN MIGUEL ARCHANGEL 1797

there is safety
in distance
from here
the storms are fifty
miles away
yet in the dark
your beloved nowhere
comes to rest
next to you
words you prayed
curl up under the covers
and there is some comfort
in feeling the blankets of morning
flesh just accepting us

ANNIVERSARY

You see, we were in the middle
of this conversation....
What love do you mean?
Where do you feel it most?
Your hair is clean and
I love that. Now where
does the rest of you
come from? The trees
are turning color
and losing leaves.
What else can we talk about?
Our fights every Sunday?
Or the nine flowers
on Wednesday?

PHOTOJOURNALIST

Where will you go after the war?
Will you listen for the fighting
in our streets, see a wreath
like a smile of flowers, hear shots
fired from room to room?

I take you to mean
our life is changing,
summer to fall. The walls
crumble toward the west
where the sun is setting
in violent, gentle red.

You will take photographs
of every attraction.
You will move your lens
toward countries in revolt,
the tortured,
or anyone
soon to be replaced.

LYRIC

Beads are you, lace is me.
You see, we have our differences
that I, at least, must claim
and make clear. You use a coupon
when I would not, ask someone directions
as I see the street we want.
Beads are you, lace is me.

MAKING A QUILT
TO COVER THE WINDOW

The sky is finished
and now she is working
on the prairie. The fabric
is layered and sown
along a horizon
imagined by many in Ohio
as ocean.

There is a sunset
off center with the blue of the sky
at the top and the brown shades of late summer
below. We follow the trail
into scattered trees
where the grass
shelters most of life.

When the quilt is lifted
exposing the glass
you see your own face
and the twisting
of cloud and water,
a storm gathering strength.
From here, anything west
is over the edge.

ANY DAY AT THE REST HOME

There is no cover for the winter wheat.
And when the winds come
in March the dry stems of grain
will break and the lines on
the ground will grow deeper
like our faces. We will watch our children
drift off to machines or mountains
to find on their own a way of life
so like ours we turn our eyes away.

Away from grandchildren who
can't stand our smell, or our tears,
or the stare that follows them
across a room. If we could smile
that too would frighten them so why not
just stink and say, "Bye, bye"
a million times to my husband
or my wife or the hand I hold tight
and kiss and kiss.

DEAR JOEL

After our phone conversation
tonight I walked the dog in the field
near our house. As I told you
we had a hard snow
coming in from the north, Nebraska,
South Dakota, North Dakota, a good
snow that stings the face
and gives light to the darkness.
Some of the grass missed by the swather
in July sways in the wind,
not a dance, just a brown
shadow of centuries of desire
and romance and revival. I hear the wind chimes
outside by the front door, I don't want them
to stop, I don't want to go to bed
just yet. I wanted to sleep out in that field
or wander around it all night. There was peace
in the cold, in the trees and I thought, what if
I fell and broke a leg, would I die surrounded
by the cold that would turn warm and by that light
from the north. I let out a quiet shout
to see where it would go. I was like the kid,
the young boy, I might have been
if I'd had a big dog, a field
and been allowed to go out late
at night in a storm to feel the sting of
the snow that was so much better than anything
that happened during the day.

GOD WON'T OVERLOOK US

THE GHOST FISH

"Stop the clocks…"

–W.H. Auden

Many friends and even my daughter
have said to me –
Just take a deep breath –

The hope is to save everything
but you don't have to look
too closely to notice

the skeleton of my body even
as small as I am.
You would not choke

on my bones although
I have required medical help
to arrive at the water

of this life. Now I am stronger
and even though you can
see through me

during this exhibit
remember what comes of
swimming in a cage.

The largest, most aggressive fish
in this tank has retreated
in its anger because it doesn't

want my taste in its mouth.
I am labeled a ghost, nearly invisible –
so I don't promise to be awake when you come to bed.

WAKING UP A DAY LATE

--Tijuana, 1999

I realize today
that my life
has been a day late
for a week.
I survived
my panic for living
the correct day.

I survived seeing
the crosses
and flowers
along the border
wall. Looking north
I realize also
that I am feasting
on your best wishes.

CHASTITY CHAMPION

You are looking for something
to do while your husband
is out of town with the team.
He is a pitcher hoping to make it
beyond Wichita, past Rochester,
but now you are both
getting ready for the winter
season in Venezuela. But are you ready
for the heartache
already in your eyes?

Chastity, you are selling beer
at this double-A stadium
on a hot summer night. You
are smart and know
the dangers of the game.

You are also pretty
with blond hair ready
to catch even the lightest
breeze. The green field behind you
is a beautiful background
for your hopes and the scattered
lightning strikes
much closer than they seem.

LAX

On an airplane I don't like to drink
more than one cup of coffee. No,
it's not the caffeine. I usually
don't talk like this
because I am shy and because
I like being anonymous
when I travel
and I hardly know you. What
is your name? Mine is Jennifer
and this is my husband, Jason.
We are going to Los Angeles, too.
We've been married eight months
and that's where we spent
much of our honeymoon, there
and Hawaii. He is a youth pastor
and has a meeting and I am going
shopping with some friends. But we
are renting a car because we'll be
there for ten days, maybe go to
Arizona to see his parents.
It's not the caffeine. I just have
one cup because I don't like
to use the bathrooms on the plane.
I'd rather go on the ground.

THE NEW ADDRESS BOOK

So many people have changed
addresses that this blue one is no longer
helpful. Most of our children
have at least three homes
crossed out. Our son has a whole page
just for himself and none of them
are current. Now he is in a ranch house
in the Texas hill country
and the beginning of a second page
in the old book.
There are some friends who have
died—Becky in her forties with a brain
tumor, Jim with a suicide, some I've just let disappear.
For a few I've done weddings,
for two their funerals: Isabel Poage and Jay Poage,
my parents. Divorced for many years
both died within three years of each other.
I was not their minister
but neither was anyone else.
I was their son and I was a pro.
So I did their funerals, threw the first
handful of dirt on similar cherrywood cremation caskets
at gravesides in Kansas
and California. Even now
as I think about what not to write
in the new address book
I fight to find space on one of the pages

to write down their phone numbers
and some street and state location
because I know they have not disappeared.

IT'S ALL IN THE TIMING

I ask if we had a meeting last week. Finding out that we
did then I ask if I was there. I am told no (!) which makes
me feel better about my mind. I also am told to check my
mailbox because the last time anyone looked it was so full
nothing could be added. I might be missing out on some
very important information. I do have responsibilities here
that must not be discounted. To discount is to under
value, proclaim the good news of a ten-percent reduction
in the value of your children or your elderly mother. When I
asked about that meeting you don't know how
much courage it took and then I had to ask about my presence.
I know everyone got a good laugh which is healthy for many
of us. I make a long distance phone call to my therapist.
I tell her I feel like I am writing from prison because I
remember the feeling of being jailed as a six year old
by my father in a military prison. Others looked at me
through the bars. I know –it was just a joke, and laughing
is good for you. I can still see my father smiling.

THE RING

Your naked hands
are proud of you. They
want to show
the world how it feels
to begin a day without
attachments to fingers
or love lost, or details
of a life repeated
and repeated until
even you throw
those hands in the air
and surrender.

LATER AND LATER

The night was on edge
when it seemed that
at any moment
we could all
slip and fall deep
into the canyon.
We could then have
a new direction
for our loneliness
and something else
to talk about.

So we jumped
and the rush
swallowed us alive.
The invisible
horizon towered
above us, waving
goodbye,
just like in a children's book
written to make it easier
when read at bedtime
for everyone to fall asleep.

THERAPY

I keep hearing the kid crying yesterday
from some place
in the building. It does

not distract me rather
it adds a strange
companionship to the afternoon

conversation. More than
a companion, more
than words

but tears,
terrified and angry,
bring the voice

into the world
with blood and shouting
like rape or sudden birth.

AUTISTIC CONTIGUOUS POSITION

Where the hell did November go? It makes me so mad
when a month has just disappeared and then I worry
that the next one is going to be gone as quickly and I won't
be able to find it. What is the purpose behind so much dis-
appearance? Where did they go and are they being tortured
as so many who are missing? Sometimes they are never seen
again and the mourning lasts a lifetime. We cannot gather
together after the official time of mourning is over for picnic
at the cemetery and tell the stories of the missing and
presumed dead. We can never be sure that they will not be
discovered in some mass grave after days or weeks, or God
forbid, years. We can never be sure that they won't walk back
into our lives long after we have settled into something new
and maybe even satisfying. Then they will try to reclaim a
long lost past as their right. They will try to touch my skin
that no longer lusts for what was so beautiful and seemed so
right but now has disintegrated into anger and grief like a
last look at the casket as my handful of dirt is released into
the grave. "Most of my creative energy is tied up in thinking
about how to make visible invisible mending." A friend sent
me those words in a letter. I keep thinking of skin as my
earlier poems even show. Long ago I was worried about my
skin and how I would or would not be touched. Now I am
going to be quiet for I'm not sure how long, maybe search for
November, or a lover, and all the while know that the silence
presumes disappearance.

THE BIRTHDAY BOY

He knew he would go blind
if he continued to write
his poems. That is like
the bloody footprints
on the dancers'
dressing room floor.

I suggest you read,
"When I consider how my light is spent"
per our conversation
about talent, discernment,
and vocation. Then continue
making more of you.

MORE JESUS PAPERS

Looking back
there were some indications
but she was such a beautiful
wordsmith
that she chose
her words carefully
like we do
early in therapy.
She did not want
anyone to know
and gave no signs.
No one was expecting this –
no one.
Her partner found her
in the car in the garage
with their dog and one
of the cats. She left
all documents in good order
like a practiced attorney
even asking for cremation.
She left a note
that I did not read
but heard that it apologized
for the pain
she was causing everyone
but the despair she was living
was more than anyone recognized.

THROAT

I don't like the taste of the blood coming from my tongue or the
sharp broken tooth I try to hide from the photographers who
think the rest of me is so soft from my feel all the way to my
black throat. And I move in the many directions that are asked
of me or suggested as the one with the beautiful skin and
mysterious eyes. I never made it in a family portrait because I
was the one always on my own playing in the dust in the front
of the house. There were ways I could make people pay attention
to me but I could not make them love me so I learned to use
my fist like a sexual tool. This is not a beautiful image. I need
some other way to imagine my life. I could ask you
but you have always been silent like an autistic child sitting in
the corner. I cannot live like that. I can only be silent for so
long and then I have to lash out, throw my glasses against the
wall over and over again, walk for hours thinking it over. The
conclusion is so often the same. I will keep running because I
can only love one at a time yet even then I have to imagine
more than one, that I am attractive to everyone and want to
look so nice in the pictures that you will desire me and all I
have to do is move in the ways asked or suggested. You have
seen me in magazines and wondered how I could be so soft
and tender because this is not the one you know. I am the one
who throws the coffee pot across the kitchen. I smile for the
camera but I keep myself stored inside until I explode and have
to guard against paralyzing my tongue so I yell, I throw my fists
at shadows pressing against my skin against my will. When I
finish, my throat is raw.

PUBLIC RADIO

Tomorrow we will interview
two organic farmers from Vermont
about who they want
for President and why.
This will be of national
importance because all across
the country all sixteen percent
of registered voters who may
get to the polls will be anxious
to hear what the Vermont
organic farmers want from the
most powerful person
in the world. So the nation
will listen, as I plan to do,
because what I hear
may effect my vote
which could then change
the course of human history
in an organic sense. Rodale Press
will be on hand to comment
and their expert pundits
will be side by side
with Larry King and the other major
networks. We will all rest more
peacefully because tomorrow will bring
out into the open, finally, the life
of the human soul. The landmines

and chemical weapons
around the world, the armies
of eleven year olds, all those civilian
casualties of contemporary
war, the nuclear missiles continually
aimed at the good earth, will once again
all be completely ignored.

THE SNOW SHOVELERS

They came, two of them,
to my front door
asking if they could
shovel the snow
from the sidewalk
and the front porch.
I asked how much.
The older and taller one
whom I presumed was
the father said 5
or 10 dollars.
I agreed. They shoveled
until the work was complete.
I paid them. I asked
the kid, ten or eleven,
where he went to school.
He did not say. I looked over
to the man I presumed
to be his father and noticed
a small gold earring.
It was simple and shone
in the sunlight
that would have melted
the snow in about ten minutes.
I paid them 12 dollars and we looked
up and down the street for other
possible jobs, other sidewalks with snow.

There were none. I talked about
the weather with the man
and noticed the sweat pouring down
the side of his neck like a river so clear
you can see the rocks on the bottom.

COUNTRY KITCHEN

"Tenderness can be just as abstract as insanity."

--David Lynch

For some reason
the waitress is very
attentive with a nice smile
and I respond
making a remark
about an item on the menu
called "Everybody's Favorite,"
and that being the case and me
not being able to decide,
I tell her yes I'll have that.
She laughs,
checks with me several times
as I eat and read
the Kansas City paper
but I'm really thinking
of my friend dying
of cancer and my tears
must be red in my eyes.

I finish the meal, still not sure
what town I am in
just because of my
towering grief like the giant
without a name. Because
I want someone to have
a good morning

I leave a five dollar tip
for a six dollar meal
knowing my financial advisor
would not approve. However,
the waitress found me
at the cashier's counter
and put her hand on my shoulder.
She said: "You are the nicest man
I have ever met." Then she turned around
to go clear off my table. I was already
in a country far away.

"Your vocation is anything
that makes more of you."

–Gail Godwin, novelist

I am not much for quotes
plastered on my wall but this one
has been hanging on the lining

of my stomach for years.
Now take this sheet of paper
for example and the words

you are reading. Do they want
to make you go out
and fall in love? Or sit quietly by yourself

in a café sipping coffee? Inspiration to go from
one day to the next is hard
sometimes to come by. In fact, I wonder how you do it.

And then I also wonder how these words appear. It is work
but it is more, a stammering from my guts, a search to find
more of me, or less, depending on some line-drawing

of myself above the sink. Did you catch the question above?
'Do they want to make you
go out and fall in love?' No, they

don't. They are merely
seeing if you
are awake and ready for your vocation.

While you decide, for or against my love, as you watch
all kinds of chances to make more of you, of us,
I will walk across the street and hope you notice me
without my disguise.

JIHAD

I walked past the Swedish Embassy
in the dark
watched closely
by security
because I am
a subversive.
I am so dedicated
to this cause,
it is sacred and soon
I will be in ecstasy,
in heaven
because I gave myself
for my god,
all of humanity,
for my family.
It is the least
I can do.
I will get as close
as I am able
with this bomb
strapped to my ribs.

YOUR FRIEND

I am writing from the edge
of what is no longer
mine. I thought I would
never come back
but through an invitation
I find myself
on the east coast
of my old place.
Many memories, many
ghosts, some familiar.
All the living are strangers.

SPIDER LIGHTNING

What I am most afraid of is coming so close to the light that
   I burn
leaving scars on my face that cause my heart's eight legs to
   dance
like the spider in the sky. Many of my friends have died that
   way. Not
because they wanted to, it was just that they could not get out
   of the way
fast enough. I am writing these words in secret because I am
   so healthy now
that even a trace of the hidden seems like a betrayal of some-
one. I raise
my fist in defiance or shadow box at midnight to defend
   myself against
the words on the subway walls that I don't even understand
   because it is a new
language developed by lovers from the recent generation.
   The alphabet of this love
cannot be arranged in ways I desire although the mystery of it,
   I must admit,
makes me at least curious and I refuse to have my curiosity
   questioned as something
dirty. So I raise my fist again. The sky ignites all over the
   horizon
and I know I am falling, falling, falling, falling, falling again.
Do not try to save or rescue me.

TAKING MYSELF TO THE MOVIES

I decide on one I have never heard of and the review
leaves me confused but interested enough to see it. As
always the closer the time comes to leaving, the more
chores I find to delay driving across town to the theatre.
It reminds me of the reluctance on therapy days and I
wonder what the connection might be. At the last moment
I turn on the outside house lights, front and back, because it
will be dark when I return. The dog, inside most of the day,
wants to go just for the ride. We rush out the front because
even though I'm doing this kind thing for myself it feels
undeserved and I don't like to be late for the start of a movie
yet I have stalled so now it takes on the feel of an emergency –
like work, so I won't feel so bad about this simple act of
freedom and pleasure. And if you are reading this poem
with even the least bit of interest or attention you have done
exactly what I did, delay your departure for wherever you
were going when you turned to this page. Do you also feel
that bad about discovering the pleasure of doing something
kind for yourself? Are you cutting it so close that it feels like
an emergency?

MEANINGFUL JOURNEYS TO END
THE CENTURY

Today I found myself
talking to my dentist about the suicide

of a friend. And then about
the handmade notebook

of one of Stalin's prisoners
with an Ahkmatova poem on one page

written from memory. What do you think
was written on the other pages?

How much despair
is too much? Poems

are a lyric revolution
giving hope even in the exile

of the soul. I can see in the distance
mountains of refuge hiding the escaped

freedom fighters. They are cold,
far away and are called the Crazies.

How much love will it take
to carry me that far?

ECSTASY

you hear the distant train
as you stretch
out on the bed
in the darkness
the air conditioner
cooling your skin
like rain
out on the street
and just by the look
in your voice
it is clear
you will soon be off
to see the music
for yourself

THE MASK

I woke up at 4 a.m. because I heard my name
called out loud from downstairs. I wanted to
get up and see who it was but that was
impossible. I was afraid and sure it was someone
close to me who could have any part of me just by
looking. Then where would I be? There was no one
else in the house and my sleep was losing hold
of all the dreams up to that moment. Then
I kept hearing the seduction and wanted to walk
carefully down the stairs in the dark-as-blood
air and follow the call like nobody's business
but mine. Remember the talking cure, the babbling safety
net, making noise just to scare away the fear and
then make my way into the first room closest
to the front door and finally she is there but I cannot
see her because my eyes are covered by the mask
that I wear upside down so my mouth is
where my eyes should be and my eyes are still in the same
old place blinded by a fearsome decoration.

MISS KANSAS TARGETS VETERANS

Don't let this news get out.
Some of us don't want
to read or write the truth.
Then, of course, we all
have questions
that truth can never
stand up to
and face eye to eye.

In your desperation
or hope you stop at the house
of a palm-reader and she tells you
there is little difference
coming in your life
but much change.
Leaving the house you notice
in your heart a rhythm
unlike your usual song.

The competition to get this far
takes a toll. You pay
because your small town
has raised money and your school
voted you queen. You wave,
smile, and vow
to end the affliction
of veterans. This country

needs more people like you,
the paper says,
letting the news get out.
The flowers look
beautiful, cradled
in your arms.

SLIPPING INTO SOMETHING COMFORTABLE

She took off her clothes.
It was that simple.

MANIC LOGIC

"With enough courage you can do without a reputation."

--Rhett Butler, Gone with the Wind

I found the perfect thing in France and nothing like it
any place else. You know
how it is when you see something that you have been
looking for just about
forever and then with a split second decision you let it go?
That's the way
I feel about that perfect thing. I have walked from one end
of this city to the other
and nothing even comes close. I have crossed all seven
bridges over the river that
divides all this hostility and wandered through
neighborhoods where the kids are
playing soccer in the streets. I have stopped at little stores
clinging to the sides
of the hills when it is nearly dark and asked if they had
what I'm looking for but
I have the wrong language in mind. I can't even use my
hands to get my meaning
clear enough. And everyone seems to think I am crazy as
I stumble through my
efforts at reaching out from my sincere heart to these poor
people who need me
to save them. And it is not because I believe I am the
messiah or have some kind
of complex. Do you know what I am trying to say?

You see, I walked into a Jewish
cemetery with landmines scattered and buried like
bodies waiting to reach up out
of the ground to pull another one of us down. I walked
off the central steps without
thinking and stood on a stone or a piece of a
gravemarker. I took pictures.
Why didn't a hand come up out of the ground, grab
my foot and rip it off?

THE DEMANDS OF THE DAY

I go to the airport even though
I am neither departing
nor arriving. It's a small
terminal with twelve gates
and flight crews lamenting
being stuck in this town
for the night. One of them,
optimistic in her life, says,
"We'll find some fun."

I stay long enough to
look at the magazines,
watch a couple of planes
takeoff into a low, overcast
sky and see people carry,
pull or drop their luggage—
how they embrace or kiss
each other, the regret
or relief on faces after
goodbye. I am an unknown
and security gets suspicious.

I leave the terminal, find
the car and drive to my bank
where everyone knows my name
and even sing "Happy Birthday" to me
on the right day because I

told them, half kidding.
I come here because I have needs
that are met and the demands
on my day disappear with each smile.
I am not afraid, thank God, of these people.

YOU GO THROUGH THESE MOODS

I've been buying flowers for myself
lately. You know I can be oblivious
to so many things around me. I know
it hurts people. But look at who
I am. Look at this freedom
glowing in my face. You reach
across the table and touch my cheek.
You could not help it, right? It felt
so warm and welcome, the invitation
was so natural. I want to be in a place
where the passing from one millenium
to the next comes as quietly
as watching a candle or
almost holding your hand.

PRAIRIE AVE., LOS ANGELES

Being the brave man you are
you've made it across the prairie
to the Great Basin. The plane lands
as one of hundreds
assigned by computers
to get everyone to the edge
of the continent. You rent the car,
cheap and blood red, then drive east
on 105, north on 605, then off
at Washington. The motel
has a king bed, coffee maker,
cable t.v., and pool. You wake
up late hoping life
has changed with the early
morning earthquake.
But it just rolled the ground
enough to make you change
positions. What has always
stalked you is in bed
with you wanting more
and more. Even your tearful
no is an invitation,
your mouth is open
and your eyes cannot
speak one more word.

"black as God"

Zaire is gone
welcome to Congo
we hang on the window
our small white flags
as if we surrender
but like the fiesta
it is really
revolution

you taste
you see
I love being God
at times like this
turning the world
around like Villa
or Che
I let my color
be known

it is a blessing
a call to bring the army
of the lord
into a last, narrow
valley of water
that will soon
be turned to blood
another favorite
biblical color

SUBTITLES

Mel Brooks is 73 today.
I thought he said, "Hopefully
he is a good Catholic person." He
actually said, "Hopefully he is a good
cabinet person." You know – more politicians are talking
about their religious faith openly
these days. I have trouble reading subtitles and looking at
their photo. I miss, and I confess this publicly, major
themes in the plot.

QUIZ SHOW

What is behind
the door of that smile?
I've just had a beer,
I'm exhauseted
mad as hell at the world
and never been happier
in my life.

No one wins money
here. In fact you
don't really win
anything. You may
be presented a gift
as if it were some
important day
but you won't win it!

There won't be
applause or that kind
of false affirmation
that lights up so many rooms on command.
This time you and I
need only to stay close,
take a deep breath,
and come up together
with the answer.

'MY LIFE WITHOUT GOD'

--former atheist

We agreed
to just let the poem
do you after giving all you had
for the day. Let the poem
hold you and touch you
in all those places that count,
that make a difference
for your life and pleasure.
Not fun, you say,
it is not exactly fun,
more like feeling deeply
engaged with a less demanding
lover at least
until the words are on the page.
Just lie there and let
the poem move its tongue
all over your skin
and the fingers of each
stanza carry you along
like the river
with water made only
for your healing.
Hallelujah, you say.
Jesus Christ!

CANCER

I can't turn dread
into bread
like the dyslexic
sign painter
at home
in Brooklyn.
This lump in my breast
is not the same
as the deliberate cold
of the Antarctic pain.
I could only treat
the deadly tissue
for so long. I waited.
It was too cold
even for snow
or wings without ice
I needed this rescue
but no life boat,
rope, or strong
grasp of a hand
is going to be enough.
I can tell by the look
on all of your faces
that you are tired
and waiting for the other
to say to me
it is time to let go.

PLACES

I drive to the places I remember
as if they still existed. Some people
look at me perhaps recognizing
something about my smile, my walk
or the way I speak certain words.
I go to the place where the theatre
stood. In second grade I went to movies
where now there are only rough grey
walls. My grandfather, the one always
seen as suspicious, the artist, painted
the original interior in Egyptian
style. Now the blue sky
is the ceiling and the wall
for the screen opens to cottonwood
trees along a creek. I bring my wife
and daughter to see this shell of memory
that encases the entire town. Here is where
my great grandfather had a bank. And up
these steps you will find the rooms
used by my great uncle when he
practiced medicine. My suspicious
grandfather presided over poker games
in the basement. He probably smoked.
We walk the streets and the alleys
where tiny tornadoes of dust
swirl around our feet
like the small words I learned

even as I listened to the radio
on a quiet Sunday night
a world away from the war
and my father's desperate courage
in the face of overwhelming odds.

QUESTIONNAIRE

In the end,
I felt like an experiment.
Here is one thing
you can try
and then you can swallow this.
Have you ever been
in love? Yes,
but so long ago
I can barely remember
what it feels like
except when I dream.
One more question: Sex?
Soft androgyne, according
to a test I once took.
I don't feel very safe now
like I am in the hands
of a dangerous person.
My skin hurts.

WELCOME TO PAWHUSKA

"Choose Joy" were the two words
on the back of the young girl's
T-shirt in Pawhuska, Oklahoma.
She was working with her family
in the business of feeding people
who wanted to get out of the house
or who could no longer
talk to themselves. This was a café
called, The Bluestem, named
for a grass growing for centuries
with good nutrition for bison
then for cattle. The young girl
had a gentle smile as she
put the chairs on the tables
legs sticking in the air
like they were frozen dead
on a nearby winter
battlefield. This small town
is the capital of the Osage Nation.
We come here from Kansas, on our own,
for a two day vacation. The Osage
were forced here from the prairie
to the hills and trees covered
with thorns. If you grab a branch
you will most likely bleed
from the wound. The young girl,
knowing the day is nearly over,

is rolling up the long black rubber
welcome mat so she can
sweep the floor, lock the door,
turn out the lights, and say no
to anyone looking to the bluestem and this land
for joy, a vacation, or a surprise
winter attack at dawn.

CHICAGO'S FIREWORKS

There must have been about four sites
sending fireworks into the sky. One
was from the top of a building
near Michigan Avenue. The four sites
exploded at midnight
simultaneously. I kept pointing
while saying look there and there
and there. The show must have lasted twenty minutes and each
minute had something new. Someone
threw confetti into the air,
so we walked home along Lakeshore
bearing sparkles on the outside
as well as on the inside. Some people,
of course, pushed. Some kids
got on top of a kiosk,
danced, wiggled, and stripped
but January 1, 2000
was not a night
to see another white boy's
skinny body.

TERRORIST

From a friend's letter to me:
I just finished reading an article
in the Times science section
about two researchers
who, in their new book,
make a case that the earth is alone
in the universe as a place
of complex life. And to me
one of the terrifying
things about any kind of suffering,
physically or emotionally—
and even in the world
(of politics) is that the rest
of the world goes on,
and will go on
regardless of what happens.
And especially in D.C.,
in the K Street corridor
where dark windowed cars
go by and everyone
is preoccupied. No one would
notice a person
being torn to pieces,
being torn away.
It's true and you can read about it
in the new book
as the case is made

for suffering alone
surrounded by life
(by body, by soul).

CRIME SCENE

The yellow tape still surrounds the house and yard
where a 19 year old man was killed early this morning.
There were three kids in the house but they were not
harmed—at least they were not shot. He was baby-sitting
his girlfriend's children and she was in the house a
half-hour before she found the body. She grabbed the
kids, ran out of the house into the rain to a neighbor
and called police. There are no leads, no motives. That
is the way it seems so often in life and in death. No leads,
no motives. We go from one weapon to another, one
rage to another, one prison to another, or maybe find
a hiding place to rest and clean off the blood caked to
our teeth. But soon we are on the run again stepping
on or across those who have fallen before us, victims
of a bribe that turned sour or some betrayal that no
one could have predicted so now we escape to the
mountains and hope gangs of thugs and militants
don't find us hiding here in the trees. Soon we will
need to light the fires to keep warm and melt snow to
make water to drink. Our allies have not come through
with the needed support. You could say that we are left
on our own, we have been abandoned to the elements
and hostile fire. The children, yes, the children—they
were left behind for someone to take care of. We hope
they are not shot or harmed in any way. Perhaps a
grandparent will keep them safe, someone my age
will take them to the basement away from the scene
of so much lying, so much deep cold, and the crimes
of home.

PIECE BY PIECE

You say that to analyze
me like taking apart
a clock is the way
you can build trust.
I admit I can be taken apart
without much effort.
Does it work both ways?
I remember when I was
a kid I would
take things apart
like clocks (or other things that moved)
and the parts
would end up scattered
around the floor in no
particular order.
I don't recall
ever getting the pieces
together again.

WHERE WE ARE

I don't want
to pound my brain
or my skin.
You and I had
something going here
in the tall prairie
grass. I could not
keep you near
though I gave you
those best years
of what I thought
was my life.

A NOTE

I am sorry
all has been so difficult
and I feel I have not
been around for you.
(Maybe that has been alright??)
I leave three weeks
from tomorrow. Much
to get done but I would
love to see you when,
and if, you have a break
(or breakdown!). I have not
decided among Latvia,
Santa Barbara, or the moon
or maybe the sun
and just melt away.

AMERICAN BEAUTY

Now it comes
down to the most
simple of pleasures
like coming to this
motel alone, getting
room 412
and leaving the
floor to ceiling curtains
open all night.
Then waking early in the
morning to the low, grey
clouds and small rain
in the silence
and chill of making
the whole thing work
for the good of
my own desire
and the recollection
of the rest that will
reassure my body
that through my choice
I am safe
and beautiful.

JUST A THOUGHT

The sky is open to flying
through itself if only
you and I can spend the time
to cover our bodies
with the fragrance of being
next to each other in more
than one instant that would
move the clocks and yet
transform time
into the rhythm of a love
that brings leg to leg,
arm around a bare waist,
lips together, and the heart
bleeding to life.

LA FRONTERA

--Tijuana, 1999

There is this round table
more solid
than our lives.

It is good
for writing the poems
that sort through

the bits and pieces
that form minutes—
hours, and

if we are lucky
or surprised
a full day.

GUARDIAN ANGEL CHANCES 50¢

for Cora, August, 1998

Not knowing what to expect
we moved slowly
through the Italian Festival.
This was Sarah's town
but not her festival.
We walked up to a table
with a sign announcing the same message:
Fifty cents for a chance
at a guardian angel.

We moved along
not asking any questions.
We had been looking for cheap birthday presents
for you, not necessarily angels,
but your sister led us out of
Italy and into upstate New York.
We walked the streets. Sarah was angry in her silence.
I stumbled over words,
the sidewalk, our broken family.

On this vacation, even on vacation,
we have noticed parents
yelling at their children on the beach –
we are all family here,
we will enjoy it,
we will do it all together!

Then it is over. We come home,
learn about the deaths
while we were gone
and I'm not sure I have
enough of the right words.
So I reach in my left pocket
hoping to find fifty cents.

GOD WON'T OVERLOOK US

I walked along the mountain ridge
and watched the lonely
strong shadows
(of a setting sun).
I have grown with the trees

holding the idea of love
around in my head
but when it came
to the kiss
the shadows spread again.

I have grown with the trees
beyond the brainstem stories

I hear in my dreams.

ABUNDANCE

THROUGH THE WINDOW THE BALLET

dancer at the pole
makes moves I cannot
name. The sun
shines on her face
and arms. I take a few
photographs of her profile.
She never turns to face
me. This is the day,
we are told, when the world
must go on. With war
only hours away
the dancer will keep
her arms and legs
moving through the air
over and over
picturing for us
all the love
that must go on.
She knows. It is her way
of telling us all
that is important like
a leaf or a hand
held in the air for
another second.
The window gives the world
a silent portrait
of dancing far beyond

death. It is forever
she tilts her head as if
to hear the whisper
of her name.

(London/Sarajevo, March 18/19, 2003)

AT THE PARK

You swing every
which way
and catch
the smell

of something
sweet in the air
but can't for the life
of you

find it. You say
it is always
this way
in the world

you know. You swing
every which way,
folding your legs
for speed,

stretching them
out for

distance, your
best friend.

THE OUTER VEIL

Consider the lilies,
an altar
sweet
as a foreign tongue.

The wise-hearted
burning blue
cords of cloth,
linen of working love,

alive in the soil,
a violet vision
of the charms
the smell of your hands.

OUTDOOR MARKET

--Sarajevo

The dust
becomes you.
The distant voices
call out to you
with words of
the body's soul
and parts.

In this country –
a corner of the world
made for love,
a bomb in the market,
and simple food –
there were still
two bodies found
by the road we are on.

We won't tell the children.
It is a political work
to keep revenge
in the family
just like our own
deadly conversations.

BALCONY

You have seen
the promised land –
touched by the sea,
swallowed the salted air –

all that makes
you fresh
and fight-filled.

You stand on the balcony
silent on the phone
waiting to believe.

CROW, MONTANA

-- for Joel

From the house
you can see
the Pryor Mountains.
Clouds give life
a steady change.
Grass across the valley
hides all that most
of us ignore every day.

Early in the morning
we hear our horses
stolen from the enemy.
We will ride them
to victory.

We dream. You see the river
swimming, moving its arms,
pushing the driftwood
like bones.
Again, it is
a dream to make
the world speak
like a rock.

WEATHER

A stray thunderstorm is possible.
Then most likely clouds
with heat and beads
of what you want. Not cheap.
But after the storm, even
as it wanders in and out
of sight, in and out of desire,
there will be light from sky to ground,
with a deadly and precise kiss
straying along all skin
exposed in open areas –
like a park or a bed of roses.

THE DIVORCE TABLE

Peel back the skin
      from the berry, watch
            the way the bird
                  does it for the pulp

of the heart

Take the evils
      of the world
            or this street
      then stretch your arms
toward the trees
            and dream of
                going it alone.

CAN WE JUST END IT?

Who would be most angry with the near
sacrifice of Isaac? That story reads as calmly
as last night's fortune: "Your life will take a turn
for the better." We have read the words over
and hoping for that sting of death
that would bring out some passion
between us. But what is most alive
is that moment when the tears almost
fall to the ground like a knife
above some important vein. Life is too short,
my father said thirty years ago.
Tonight I said the same words, here on the prairie,
walking the dog, not holding hands with you,
just talking. Life is too short to let the anger
live any longer in this heart. After all there is always God
to blame or Abraham. Or maybe it takes
both of us to hold the knife and do it right.

THE LIST

Getting older means
running out
of people you want to be.

This morning
you have been crossing
names off a list
you've never
shown me.

You talk about your health
and who you really are
beneath the southern, very
beautiful skin and
eyes that change color
with mine. Anyone watching
us together would
write our names
down.

DAKOTA

The willow tree
in the backyard
moved with
my eyes. It was
full of hope
and courage,
teaching me
like a grandfather,
a wise one
not drunk
with thirsty hands.

I lied. There was no
tree, only the endless
sky and always
the wind,
or thirst,
caressing
my long, soft
girl's hair.

PRIME TIME

I am not sure
what more I can
say to you.

Last night
I had a dream
that I left
the headlights
on. I looked
out the window
and saw them
slowly fading out.

GRATITUDE

The sun is blinding
as it drops down
into my childhood sea
where waves surface
like the animals I draw
and tape to my wall.

Soon, very soon, every
corner will be dark
and in my room
I will sing.

IN THE KITCHEN

You have been
reorganizing
your recipes,
alone,
like a
fatherless
woman,
loving so much
the desert island
music.

THE MAGI

Fair is fair.
So what does
that mean?
You have been
chewing on those
questions for years.

Soon you get up, 3 a.m.,
walk away
from the bed,
and step outside
to find some other
important star.

ENTIRE ROUTE NORMAL

Each night
I hear the man and woman
next door as
their lives
become less and less.

The tide washes up
close to their feet.

Their ocean view room
has turned to salt
and the taste

no longer adds spice
or flavor but has become
so normal that
the habit is selling

for much more
than it is worth.

TRIO IN KANSAS

The bassist wore
bowling shoes, the drummer
closed his eyes, the piano
player reached sounds

pulled out from
between the keys. They played
standards – the best
"Somewhere Over the Rainbow" –

the piano solo moving
down your back,
across fields of wheat,
someone to watch over you.

CARL

You did not come here today
to preach, it wasn't in you.
Nothing much was left,
You showed me some money
in your wallet. Today
you seemed like the ghost of your regular self,
maybe you have died and are making an apearance
for my sake. You talk about
going home but the usual speed
of your conversation makes listening
a difficult game of catching up.
You expect that four thousand dollar check
tomorrow, last month, twenty years
ago. Oprah has called
and she says you'll be on a show
anytime now. You don't have the knife you often
carry or the spirit, the holy ghost,
that makes you lie down in the middle of the street.
You haven't seen your father in forty years
and never talk about a mother. Never!
Never talk about a mother. The street
is the gospel and it is hard news
to swallow anymore. I ask you
where you slept the last few nights
and I see your first tears. I ask again and you walk
toward the door to leave. You put your arms
around me and bury your head

in my chest. You are holding me,
I am holding on. Where did you sleep
these last few nights? We are now
out on the concrete porch.
I slept here, you say. Here, on the porch?
No, I slept here, and you move one hand
and place it on my chest
where underneath a sweater and a shirt
my heart would ordinarily have survived quite well.

THE CLOUD

The cloud gathers
its small rain.
In breaking
it falls to
the ground
appearing to most
of us as love
lost on the gravel road
in a downpour
that is violent
and blind.

HALF-WAY TO CHINA

You stand along the road
and watch every
passing car. No help
needed here. No outstretched
hand or
gesture of desire
or inch of your brain
could ever make
your rain-soaked,
old-man skin
warm to the idea
that this world
wants you around
anymore.

MUSIC

You take the side
of the bed
farthest from the phone,
next to the window.
It is open
even in winter
for air and to hear
the trains, the rhythm
of an iron life.

JESUS, THE BANDIT

The road is familiar as it drops
down from Jerusalem like a scar
toward Jericho. You have left family
and faith behind in the city
in favor of the dust wrapping your face
like gauze. It was a hasty decision,
impulsive your friends told you. You ignored
all the "don't-burn-your-bridges" advice.
The landscape has settled over you
as the lover of your choice
unbuttoned a smile and you agreed.
Christ!!
And you agreed.

NOT MAKING LOVE

Mulch is good
this time of year,
past independence,
before dog days,
for keeping moisture
in the soil and the plant
from dying and dying –
the breath no longer
seen in the air,
disappear, disappear –
it will be good
this time of year.

ENTROPY

Fists
like pianos
beating the bed,
the black side
of the mirror.

One body
from the night
or the sky
sharing
your wings,

Every poem
a skull
yellow as the breath,
arms in the air
life-like.

FLIGHT 50 TO PARIS

She brushed
her teeth in Detroit,
put on her
face in
New York,
a face shining
like a dime,
just like
a dime.

INTERNATIONAL DATE LINE

What happened tomorrow?
It is quiet
while she makes a drink.
The children are watching
each of us from
across the line.
All along the horizon
evening swallows fall
into angry sleep
hoping every day
will feather the next.

FROM WEDNESDAY CAT'S JOURNAL

--Riga, Latvia

"The dream last night."

That was it.
No memory of
what took place,
not details –
nothing.
The final product
is not her forte.
Now she is
warming herself
in the window
on a day when the sun
appears. It is, of course,
Wednesday.

ANOREXIA

You were naturally
attracted to strange –
lunch break at the cemetery,
hair the color
of joy, diet coke
and celery for guests.
Out of the left
corner of your eye
you could see
the skeleton
you had made
for yourself –
so it's not surprising
all that has happened.

MORNING

He put the new coffee on top of the old,
dusted the toaster with the dish rag
and sat at the table where he could find

some space. Yes, that was the hope for
a new day, some space to hear, think,
spell an old word or read a final

sentence of a novel. The forecast keeps
changing. Snow. No snow. A look at the
headlines gives the old bold print

clear statement of the day: "GUILTY!" is
the word for the world and with the
help of caffeine and toast, no jam,

no money, he'll get by. Even when
a sentence changes person or tense
that one word will get him out

the door and into the controversy
of weather. There will be more
people than he wishes to see,

more wind than the dark of early
morning could handle but the word
for the world will get him by

even though it comes from yesterday's
paper from which today he happily
reads his five star day horoscope.

LITHUANIA

The people on
the paper money
have seen their children
murdered over
and over again.

So this is
the currency, the way
to do business,
to purchase what
I want

but it makes a strange
exchange of life
for life, death for death.
The paper just falls
into other hands.

MAN FROM BANJA LUKA

He could not recall
details although no one asked.
He stood holding his hands
trying not to touch his face
knowing he would find only bone.

He sang a prayer from his
Mosque and on his knees
east was any direction except
home. It was, he was certain,
with family still inside, burning.

HERCEGOVINA

First of all
I was not born here.
I listen to the music
and want to move
in a way that gets the eye
of the boy from Mostar.
He has a knife
tucked in his belt.

I was born on the 16th of September,
1986. My family is not big;
brother, mother, grandmother,
grandfather,
and father. A big dog.
I like to swim and out
of school I like to
play in the theater.
Do you understand?
I like to play
in the theater.
I want the eye
of the boy from Mostar.

HOPE

for Anna

this catches you
in time
break a leg
and cheers to
hope and love

give me a call
if you can
folks are in town
life is busy

lots of love
out there
like I said
or you said

hope the present
arrives in time

TWO ITALIAN DREAMS

I.
Out of five one daughter
had died and there was no
relief from the loss. Never knew
which daughter the entire
night. Much of the dream
was a blur without
any detail. I was sure
only of the father's anger
by his song.

II.
At an opera I tried
to find the right view.
One place I could not even see
the stage only
hear the music.
Everything was sad. Someone
continued to move me
into other sections of the theatre.
It went on forever
from one place to the next
never getting a clear view
of the actors, scenery, lights
or who brought that broken
voice into my morning bed.

THE SIEGE OF SARAJEVO

--for Dzevad and Lida

You were caught
preparing to extend
the appearance of grace.
It will not depend
on the dead
you hold in your arms.

The river that flows
through this city
was blood
but it gave hope
of life or limb or proof
of refugee photos.

Now you may let
some children cross
the street and a woman
or two but then
as you know
they become targets.

Aren't they all our
children? Yes, but
only by appearance
and that does not
depend on the dead
one you hold in your arms.

THE HISTORY OF TIME

--for Stephen Hawking

Imagine even attempting
to write on the subject
of Time? Give us an accounting
of where you spent
last night or, better yet,
how long it took you.
It's hard just to get
the arms of my own words
around such a concept.
All I usually can come
up with are some lines
that reveal a moment
when I was breathing
with some ease
and then, without warning,
as I am driving along
some originally safe direction
I turn the corner
and see a sign that reads:
This road ends in water.

VAUDEVILLE

I don't open
and I will not close
the show. You can
dance around me
all you want
and bring on the jumping dogs
and contortion queens
but I will sing
and tell the joke
of a lifetime
so I can be
next to last
and the star.

GETTING OUT

When father died
he left so much behind –
a son and daughter,
a wife to share
drinks and anger,
grandchildren known
and unknown to him.
His first wife's grave
in Kansas.
No money.
A nearly empty
apartment.
A framed collection
of medals for courage
and getting out alive.

Another woman
claiming he
had promised all of this
to her.

BLIZZARD OF TWO

--after Mark Strand

It was not your holiday.
The marriage ended
as the snow
moved across the brown
pasture and your heart
became your face.

You yielded to your eyes
body on body.
Love like a knife
was the gift.

Now the starlings make
their home in the trees
as December
as today
as cold
settles in.

THE WAVE

--for Marina Tsvetaeva, 1892-1941

Light hides so much,
everyone's best behavior
but not the death
of drowning.

So the dark
reveals again for you what life cannot
hold back
or revive.

OLDER

You may want to let the loss
do what it will.
The fire kills at first
but soon with rain
some small life returns.
It is different, though,
you say.
True, in reply.
All you have lost
is changed forever
into a remembered walk,
a record-setting winter,
a song.
No matter.
You won't forget.

PRAYER

So wonder now about what is next.
You seem to have many
of the right questions
unlike the rest of us.
Then there is always
at least a mock interest
in answers. You listen to them
with the same excitement
as the international
weather report. Temperature
above average in Athens, cloudy
with late sun in Rome,
unusual cold and rain in
Santiago. All the information you need
to travel the world,
let alone heaven.

THE FLU

The Abbess, my new calling.
Or was it
abyss?

Sore throat. Muscles
aching. My vocation
losing it's life.

A sneeze. A cough.
I fall. Does everything make more sense
with a fever?

CONVERSATION AT THE BAR

Cold?
Not right now
but it's in the air.

They say snow, although…
Never really sure,
fifty-fifty around here.

That last snow I lost
my daughter, slid under
the car in the driveway.

And you were driving?
I can't get over it.
just going crazy.

How old?
Five and a jewel.
I see her all the time.

And hear her?
All the time.
All the time.

And always cold?
I'm always cold.
It's more than just the air.

CARNATIONS

You can't remember nouns.
And regarding carnations
you believe

that any flower
lasting that long
must have something

wrong with it.
Or maybe not.
Either way
to what end?

HAND TO HAND

--Sarajevo, 1992-1995

The front line moves every day, hour by hour,
up the hill, through another home,

across the river. This street, the alley.
A tree. A window. A widow. The enemy gives

its word one minute and the next
we pay no attention to any promise

and the world we knew lies
broken like a bone at our feet.

Families gather to give a final
song but in this place the safe ones

have lyric deep beyond our hearing
buried as a body cradled

in the snow. It looks like
someone we knew – maybe

next door or smiled at us across
a room. The fire now burning

is the warm lover brought
in a hurry as if this flame will die.

INTERVIEW WITH NICOLE KIDMAN

If you have advice
I could use it now, Charlie.
Yes, about the future,
I would want....
Well, this is very personal.
I would want
what I thought I had
all those other years.

But you will, right?
You know that.

Charlie, we never really
know anything, do we?

THE STORY OF LIFE

You could attempt a rundown
of everyone's activities. Looking
out the window you see children
getting on the morning bus,

then across the street you notice
a small dog running inside
the fenced yard. You know
from close examination

about the scar just above the eye.
But which eye? There is that
failure of remembering
again just like last night

and the dream of someone sleeping
next to you. There's been no one there
for years but you decide the crumpled
sheets give you something to make up.

GRACE, PERIOD

Sometimes girl
I just want
to send
him on his way
but then
who would love this

VOICE OVER

PART 1

LIFE JUST HAPPENED YESTERDAY

So where in the world are you?
Where have your nerves taken you
today? Why do you take off your earrings
when you talk to me?

When you moved to this city there was a storm.
When you left, the same.
The lightning was bright on the street
and the thunder pounded like fists
on the wall. It means there is more
than weather to live with.

There are all of those questions
like when will they ever find out
for sure when a storm is coming? Or not?

The windows are open and we hear
the noise of the street and the neighbors
and those who are not neighbors.
It's some kind of religious holiday
that no one understands but we all join the prayer:
"Sweet chariot, slow chariot, swing low, take us home."

In bed we watch television, the latest news
of the capitol city being taken over by the rebels.
The red cross ignored. Children with machetes
swing low. Red flags marking land mines and the dirt

carefully moved by those who still live
searching for those who did not.

Life just happened yesterday.
So where in the world are you?
I am holding in my hand some dirt
and your beautiful earrings.

COMPOSING FROM SECOND THOUGHTS

In a simple way
your spirit just
disappeared

shattered like the bones
in your small hand
that fell to pieces

into the water
as from a mid-air collision
or other if only.

TERM VS. WHOLE LIFE

"...we all deserve to wear white.

-Annie Savoy

Coming down from the tree of marriage
With daylight breaking
There is a voice at the table
Where last night's talk
Was crowded. Carry your eyes soft
As green wheat from a distance, carry
Them across the sky into the traffic
Of legs and Los Angeles faces
From the Midwest where you were assured
A life. But we all make mistakes.
Then why is forgiveness so rare? Why is the last
Speaking part already taken? You don't love
TO hear the stories anymore. Where you work
People all around you beg to die, let them,
Give them one wish. Time doesn't weigh heavy
On my hands. Yes it does. From
The Smithsonian magazine I have just read
The following: "For the first time
We are getting baseline information
On just how sensitive people really are."

THE TEARDROP GARDEN

Speaking of the truth
I sometimes have another voice
Here in Golden Gate Park
still warm from the sun
we could be serious about the song –
"No Regrets" – or we could laugh
in other directions, remembering the Thai
restaurant as narrow as the tears
on your face and mine. We walk the maze in the garden
speaking of the truth and all the while
thinking this warm sun is too good
and already how this sentence
is too long or I've done something wrong
like walking the stations of the cross backwards
starting with the burial.

EMERGENCY

The river that runs through the heart
of this city is now a center for shopping
and a good place to eat. But where is the ocean, that one
wilderness no one can speak for?
It has its own voice
learned before language was allowed.
as we think about this together we hear
the sirens of emergency vehicles.
They are going to try to rescue someone,
bring them back to life, stop
the bleeding. Or maybe
there has been an attempted escape
to Mexico after a brush with death –
so much fear painted on their face,
so much hope painted on the border sign: "WELCOME"

We stop for lunch along the river.
There is a menu special that sounds good
to both of us. Imagine something that simple?
The sirens have faded away. The wound,
the rescue, the attempted escape are all taking place
beyond our silence. This is a good
Place to eat. But where is the ocean
no one can speak for? The river knows
where it is going and soon will arrive
to a celebration of loud music and a welcome embrace.

HOLIDAY PARTY

We laughed
at all those people
we knew were much more
pretentious
than ourselves. Then returning
to Brooklyn we ended up
on a line that was not working
so we went all the way
to Coney Island, took the bus
back to Ocean Ave. to Parkside
and walked.

The clouds were thick
with light
and the new Balkan war.
Christmas came
on Monday and then a message,
perhaps from angels,
about so many regrets
for living just a quarter
of a century.

Today I tried
to find graves
for three people, unable to pay
for their dying. The New Year came
on Monday. Somewhere
there must be
more laughter.

NEIGHBORHOOD WATCH

A hit and run accident
in the street outside,
of course, outside –
hit and a hit, and a hit.

A man was seen running away
holding his head, not stopping the blood,
not healing the wound. The car
was towed away.

Somewhere the man is still bleeding,
still wounded still running
down the street,
turning a corner,

clumsy in his pain,
blurred in his vision.
And like the car
a total loss.

GOING FOR A WALK

I look out the window
of my office
and see a woman

covered with a white shawl
over a full black dress.
Her face is hidden.

In her hand
is the hand of a small child
walking beside her.

The child's coat
is like any I might have found
for my daughters

at her age, colorful
and with a hood bouncing out
of rhythm with the walking.

ORDINARY FLOWER

So much is so old.
The ordinary flower
on the table
curling up at the edges,
the yellow petals
turning brown.

It's time to leave
all of this. I am in my car
driving as carefully as I can
with the grass singing
and a hawk flying
at eye level next to me.
The sky is like an ocean, a life,
lost and blue.

I arrive at my destination,
my new city. Hoping for a new start
as I stand on the sidewalk I hear these words:
"Hey, lady. Are you looking at your forehead?
Are you looking at the blood in your bones?
Hey, lady."

RULES FOR THE USE OF RARE MATERIALS

Today you are reminded of how life
cuts the stone into shapes
regarded by some as lovely
like so many of the photographs.
You walk across the grass
and stand on the dirt of a fresh grave.
Even your tears cannot convince
whoever holds that dirt in place
to be more understanding.

There was news this morning
on the television of nothing we can do
anything about. The anchorwoman, dark hair
and professional, did not seem to mind.
But you do. The rules have been broken.
Comfort care was really
a three-day goodbye. Rare materials
have been taken for granted.

Across the road from all these cut stones
and imaginary trees, in this December air
when the sky is on your shoulders,
your mother's farm
has been planted with wheat
for a winter's life.

LAST FREE EXIT

Her legs were singing.
Her life to this point
brought the usual glances
and the less usual
happiness. Most of her friends
had given up, having done all they could.
The wind from the south
made her feel warm and, at times, hot and good.
But she needed to get off now
just as all the voices had told her.
"Get down off the cross," they said,
"we need the wood."
The familiar voices came from the women
she loved, touched, feared, wanted.
"Take this exit," they said.
"It's the blessing of freedom,
It's your song."

PROJECTED DISTORTION

What I heard were these words –
"Butter wouldn't melt in her mouth."
This group of parents talking
about their children, how they've all gone
to family therapy. Most of us in the restaurant
could hear each word. How one
daughter was so sweet and, maybe, would live
with him if they all agreed. Another sentence
went like this – "I just packed her things
and set them on the front porch. She was crying
and all that but she was learning." Another voice
said – "I appreciate you
telling me that story." Then they talk about music but their
songs get sour. "The spare bedroom," one says, "is empty
if someone wants it tonight."
Grab the melting children before they disappear, before
their parents can call the cops, escape out the back door,
then drive south across the Golden Gate.

MARATHON DANCE

Help the last one standing.
Move toward me in the shadow
of the dance, the prairie music

and a kiss returned.
Help the last one standing.
With tears and war

outside the door, our bodies ache
for a new position.
Help the last one standing.

In some Italian step
We help the last one dancing
and pay for our intimate move.

AFTER HOURS SPIRITUAL HELP

Why does the willow weep?
He stands there next to the river
as if last night's sleep
was painful, as if this Valentine's Day
was any different than the next.
Funny how we think that way
sometimes. Then he tastes the wine no one
else will taste and hears sounds not even a dog
would catch and the violent dreams begin
before sleep comes over him. The street
below the window does not show much love
so he remains by the river
and says all the mean words he can think of –
many not even in books – says them to himself
but loud enough for neighbors
who soon close their windows. It is late
after all. The curtains remind him of skirts
he watched years ago, white and flowing with the breeze.
The window is walking toward him
twirling those skirts
wanting a seduction
scene. And this is only the beginning,
a prelude he does not want.

ELY CATHEDRAL TOUR

A pursued woman
maybe 7th or 8th century
prayed for blindness
then for healing.
After getting both
no one is sure
where she is buried.

VOICE OVER

She was often the subject
of mostly loving stories
of life and death. But sooner
or later it all had to come out
into the open, it had to ripple out across the water
breaking the surface of love and running
away. Now coming in above
the Potomac River, turning this way
and another way, the pilot
brings her down within seconds
of schedule. The cab is waiting,
she remembers – take the first one in line
or they yell at you. Why did it matter?
Everyone, it seemed, was yelling all the time.
Into traffic, across the river, the driver
was saying something into his hand.
His passenger was full of questions. She
had it in her heart that she was always wrong,
always doing something wrong. She felt like a child.
Now she could not even speak
the language of the driver. Her only hope
was a postcard she brought to show him
her destination. Why didn't he drive faster,
or slower? She wanted to be alive
when she got to the museum
called holocaust.

ST. CHAD

So you have a place
in history which no one
cares about or pretends
to honor. You have a day
on the calendar but no area
of expertise.

After praying over the dead
twice this week
your tongue twists
around words that have
so little meaning – or,
more frightening, so much.

PART II

QUESTIONNAIRE

In the end,
I felt like an experiment.
Here is one thing
you can try
and then you can swallow this.
Have you ever been
in love? Yes,
but so long ago
I can barely remember
what it feels like
except when I dream.
One more question: Sex?
Soft androgyny, according
to a test I once took.
I don't feel very safe now –
like I am in the hands
of a dangerous person.
My skin hurts.

MELODY

We are getting to the age
where close friends have already died.
We talk of retirement
and grandchildren. Someone
mentions living wills
which sounds like a contradiction.
So we look at the cloudy sky
and decide to continue
our study of music, the theory,
the melody. Then
I think of Mozart, dying so young,
dumped in a hole
for the broken. But mostly
I remember, like it was yesterday,
his music and the way
he completed sound.

SATIN STREET

Her life is so different from mine
that I can't even live it

vicariously. It's like
trying to read a novel

in another language.
I recognize some of the words

but I don't know
how they go together.

Then the angel appears
outside the dream.

All I am looking for
is Satin Street,

not anxiety but a soft touch,
a kind of home.

Pushed back into the dream
I feel more danger

like preparing for a fight. But her life
is so much different than mine

And when we talk and I mention
The white horse I could be

for her even that is never heard.
The words split in so many parts

as I try to be the mother
no father could be.

I come to a dead end street
and see the angel, with long hair

down her back. This detail
is important. It makes the whole

picture much clearer. It feels now
like being a church

but it is not feeling safe.
The country in this dream

does not like the church,
its struggle, its songs.

Satin Street, satin doll, not even
vicarious. Then the dream is over

in an instant. I awake to go swimming
before work and taking the towel

to wipe the dream from my face
I remember trying to be

the mother
the father could never be. Afterall,

we both live
with purple hearts.

CAFÉ

She's back in her
pre-China routine,
back to familiar language,
disruption of lovers,
the gift of morning.
But the sky's anger
is bright. This storm
has a long memory.

DETROIT, KANSAS

The only real danger
is made by the wind,
the lay of the land,
and the train some kid
used to watch
because it was the only mystery in town.

And it still is
except for the man and woman
who come in the bar
and never talk
as if they were anonymous
in the city with the big name.

MAGIC

Your words are distorted
and the publicity
photos make you
into the magician
that you are not.
No matter that you
swallow fire,
pull birds from bright cloth,
and save yourself,
just in time,
from drowning.

Did you ever really believe?
My heart can only write
on paper.
Some of the words are even yours
and some are not. But this note
is not the result of a hidden formula
or a reading of the cards.
Beneath the surface
something pushes
against my back and chest.
I am pregnant again. You might get the word
on the street, you might get lucky,
just as they lower you into the water,
showing the audience
the chains and locks, the impossible escape
from certain death,
once more.

A RESTAURANT I HEARD ABOUT

The food there is tall
just right for a celebration,
a quiet, trembling
sort of celebration
with no family, maybe a friend
or two.

It was the kind of place
you don't want to leave.
Then you think: What a beautiful way to be.
But because of the flood held back for years
you are forced, even though they are your tears,
to higher ground – quiet, trembling, holding all you own.

STORMS TONIGHT AFTER 5 A.M.

What does it mean
to be held
in the palm of your hand?

A disciple
can take just so much
love

before the storms
of early morning
begin to drown even the best of us

and the rain, thunder,
and the snow all come hard
like death in most any family.

When you called on Valentine's Day
the recorded message ended
with: No reason to call back.

TIME

There is a burden in the air today.
It is hard to put into words
but the day has that feeling
like a lost promise

mourned. She asks you
about the difference
between dying and moving
to another state.

It is still goodbye
and who stays in touch
once our arms
have released each

other. You say
I've always been good
at experiencing happiness.
Well, not always, now and then

there are nights or days when my heart
pleads for time away.
So now you are leaving
and that is not what I

dreamed could happen.
So maybe a part of me

is relieved. I can spend
hours making plans,

buying flowers
and putting them in my
favorite places. Once
our arms have released

each other
and we are out of touch
I will sing a song but for now
I am just out of time.

WHISPERING LANE

A woman screamed from her porch.
I watched her
from my yard. I watched her
during a Virginia afternoon
of sunshine and hot streets.
I was barefoot and growing up.
I don't know who helped her
but it wasn't enough.

I was so young
and my odd language was limited
to the good stories. I could not
imagine the crib, the sleep
even a mother could not disturb.
The screams turned to whispers
in the humid air. Then no air
at all. Like a stone-cutter I've tried
to shape that woman again, tried
to write a miracle story
with gospel meaning.
After thirty years
I still want to give us all another chance.

AMPUTATION

It takes years to build up
the kind of courage you need
to go to that particular theatre – the one
that shows those difficult films
like Breaking the Waves or The Piano.

You knew what the anger would do,
the meaning of the axe, the loss
of how the world saw you,
of the silent desire
finally naming the attraction
no one dares watch
like some hideous death. But it's not the blood
you said –
just the thought of mutilation.

It takes years to build up the kind of courage
to say I am moving on or to name what you are losing.
Last night's sleep was painful, then came morning.
It takes years of slow courage to move
what has been taken away, those parts of you,
to feel what is missing.
Soon you will take a long look in the mirror.
Full-length.

"FORETHOUGHT OF GRIEF"

W. Berry

I've washed the sheets
pillow case
listened for the phone
stood by the window
watching the cars
on Main Street after
the football game
I think I'm waiting
for snow

CELEBRATION

I've done the cleaning,
put out the Halloween candy –
I've been here, and there, and all around.

I bought flowers that will soon fade.
And good scotch that will last forever.

That man who waved,
I wonder who I was supposed to be.

THE EMPTY BOOK

The clouds are moving in
with me. The forecast
is for rain on the edge of winter.
Remember in your empty book
the silent pages
speaking of your fear
as you were chased
by young men
through the narrow
streets of Jerusalem.

Now, across the bay,
you look for a way
to keep warm. You sweep
the floor, play music, read
the empty book.

There are more words
on the way. They are printed
on your hand like a secret
phone number. You will wash
but you will not disappear.

HOMELESS

Standing against the building
watching nervous people move along the street
in some thoughtless grief
or numb cadence of soldier courage
we smoke and listen to those
who would save us. But no religion
will work, no spirit in this temple
will be welcome so it is back
to elegies and above ground cemeteries
here in Louisiana that turn out
to be the real thing.

Then we are told to go to work
and earn some kind of living
so we can prove our independence
and worth but soon – very soon –
5 billion years or so – we'll lose
the sun, and then we'll all stand
next to other stars, a new ceiling,
unlimited, going forever into itself
finally bringing with it a new
and simple way to breathe, to live,
to stick the skin, and a new idea about water
and drowning, and then salvation will really burn
us up and soak us down to the bone
in sweat and we'll move
with that soldier courage down the street
a block or so and finally sleep
curled up on iron or stone.

BAZAAR

Pinkston, Dudley "Slim," 84,
cowboy, died Monday,
March 9, 1998. Service
11 a.m. Thursday,
Brown-Bennett-Alexander
Funeral Home,
Cottonwood Falls.

Survivors: companion,
Isla Swift of Matfield Green,
daughter, Beverly
of Bazaar,
sister Maxine
of Cottonwood Falls. Memorial
has been established
with Bazaar
Ladies Aid.

PART III

MIDDLE EMMA CREEK

What do we know about your world?
We know you swim hard
each morning to put oceans
between your self
and the rest of us.

We know that tonight
is one of those nights
when you drive past
the airport and feel
that urge to
go to long term parking
then to the ticket counter
of some airline
and ask – Where are you going tonight?
Since you are running
errands how about one
to Los Angeles or Seattle.

We know that to try
to keep even the minimum
of three
points of your body
against the rock wall
may not be possible
especially if the creek
rises.

THE CHOCOLATE MOUNTAINS

I am not all bone –
but you don't know
how I stay so thin.

I look at myself
in the mirror
and say –

This is who I am
with muscle and manners.
Then I take off my clothes

to prove the truth
of what I said,
to view the body

that is like no other.
And I see the possible
fault lines

and storms coming
over the face
of the ridge

and then the avalanche
and, finally, the immense quiet
after everything is buried.

VOYAGE

Today it is important
to visit the sun.
That means going out of this room
and perhaps seeing people. Then
I will have to make a decision.
Do I cross the street
or face whoever comes
along? Today, in the kitchen,
I heard on the radio
That Voyager 1 – originally sent
to observe Saturn, and those beautiful rings
out by themselves in all that color –
is moving at 39,000 miles per hour
away from us, perhaps toward some other life.
It has a Motown record with it and now
has gone farther than any other object
sent from earth. I feel like that –
I feel like I am between lives
and hope to be
in my new one soon.

RHYTHM AND BLUES

A car or two on the street now,
no voices. Naturally you stand beside the window,
your skin tight as temporary glass.
Your hands, thirty-four years old,
press against the wall
like the spiders of childhood.

You hold yourself so tall
and expand inside me and begin your song.
Time will heal and the children –
they'll be with me.

Large military bombers
practice out over the pasture
because no one lives in this desolation.
They seem to crawl along the sky
just above the dying ones
they never see. When you leave today,
leave today.

BRIDGE CLOSED _____ MILES AHEAD

Should we guess the number that is missing?
We are told the road ahead
is normal but so often
the only thing that gets our attention
is the pain. It is then
that we ask, who are we,
what is going on?
How far do we have to go
to find a bridge
not washed out,
one strong enough to carry
us across? Your exhaustion
may be the only energy you have.
Or the rage…maybe the rage
will save you. Perhaps we
spend too much time
looking for the right bridge,
fighting the road with so little sleep.
Perhaps – and take this only
as a suggestion – the rage
in your bones, in your eyes,
in every muscle –
all that hurts so much –
is the very bridge that will carry you
into the arms that are still open
and wanting to hold you.

AGRICULTURAL REPORT

I don't like to see
September end. With less than one hour
left of this month
there is time to look back
and find what was so good and what was lost.
No, maybe there is not the time
nor the words, the beautiful words.
But say there is no snow
this winter, nothing to cover the wheat.
Imagine trees shining with ice
like some holiday, a veined maple face
frozen against the window.
Mother says: "It will be all right."

Cattle are always testing the fence
like all the prayers we say
hoping to move God.
It seems we've left September
behind and now it's time
to close each window in case mother
is wrong.

STREET CORNER

The last three movies we have seen
have been difficult. Now back out into the city
you stand closer to me than usual. It is new
to be this tender. People look at us and think
we are in love. Some passion is shaped forever
by what is gone. You put your arm around my waist.

Near the church
on 38th Street
two young women
enjoy their time together. Near
our apartment we watch
a car pull up to the curb,
the door seems to automatically open
for the tall blond.
She is working our street.
We always see her on this corner
and not knowing her name,
we usually just watch for
the Monday car or the Saturday car.

Do you want to talk about the last
movie? Or why the sudden
affection? We need some answer
as the tall blond is driven away.

ASTROLOGY

I have the mystery of Virgil,
ancient history, to speak about
to my class. But the light
keeps tossing and turning me
until I can no longer
say what I want. The world
is so much safer now
but the urge to do something wrong
is still with me. The natural hostility
I've just read about is calm
and quiet but I am floating,
sinking, lofty, spirited, dangerous
with laughter. These are strange nights,
guided only by stars and how they move in the sky –
how we read their signals
and make our way
slowly to that first pain of longing
to see what might have come next.
I remember falling for you.

DROUGHT

This green August
gives no thought
to dying farms

lost in the love
of dust and harvest.
The clouds

roll and build above the mountains,
above the eye. Even in a good year
you accept no words

or touch from me.
This rain needs you.
It has been a long time
in the sky.

THE WAY IT ALL STARTED

The night began with white orchids
and the usual ice storm
for this time of year. The orchids were safe
inside on the glass-top table, small,
simple, elegant. But other life was not
that lucky. And that's what it takes
so often – blind luck.

Question: Why do you call it blind?
It's like saying – a brush with death.
What do you mean? Death is more
than a brush, luck is more than blind.

All of this is too beautiful
and too difficult. I watch the ice on the lake
move toward Michigan even though
it will never make it. From the window
there is life without white orchids
but from the sixteenth story
in the dark it is dangerous
because the love we have not mentioned is blind.

REMAINING QUESTIONS

Where did I learn to think
before speaking? The sun dies in the window
and along the horizon the glow of life
holds on saying: "God won't wait much longer."
There is no way to do it all over. Our unquiet mind
will make it crazy here tonight as I remember
your eyes that were grey but not weak, the sponge
on a stick to moisten your lips, no more liquids
because there were no more veins. I could feel the prairie
on your arms and see dust storms of the depression
across your face. Did you have some
simple wound? Who would even want to do it over?
My heart writes what it can on this paper.

HEART AND DRESSING

We enter a café
with the above title
on the menu. Hats
turn toward us
telling everyone where to buy
seed or tires
depending on whether you are staying for good
or getting out.

After coffee we go outside
to the clear sky
and stars on the street.
You ask,
"Is the moon glued to the sky?"
I cannot answer such a question.

IMAGES RECEIVED THIS MORNING

1) Her hands I imagine
   to be frequent and soft.
2) We forget the weeping
   at the well.
3) The blood is the same color
   for all our wounds.
4) The broken heart found
   in the alley.

The above list may be confusing.
There is a story and many poems
with each one. But I am tired,
so I'm asking you to find
your own words – your own
well, blood, and alley.

That leaves only one.

A POIGNANT CHINESE DINNER

It began as a simple farewell
to friends, to us. But a quiet lilac,
a purple bouquet, would have been nice.
I could have placed it in the corner
on the oval table. Instead, we made things up
About leaving, who would be missed
so much, the meaning of life
and culture. I was told I have a strange
way of using chopsticks. The evening
changed after that. We left intending to go
home for an early departure into the sun. But for the sake
of a little more fun
we stopped for drinks, rather, you stopped
for drinks and pool. Still caught, I have to keep
some of my secrets. I am afraid to say
much more. You know I smoked and drank
too much. It was just a simple farewell
but remember who got us out the door
and down the road toward real happiness.

1017 RANDOM STREET

The grass around the house is brown and broken.
The porch has been used as a chapel for years,
generations. Prayers for those dying or born
or ill with fever can still
be heard. The mountains
you don't see
have been moved by faith. The day
is so long.
The woman in the doorway
carries a child
from some danger
like November. Her smile
is almost real. Then she walks
up to me as if I can do
something about it.

She says, all these years hanging around
my shoulders, she says,
all these years,
she says, reaching out her hand, all these years, she says,
like they were her first words,
all these years, she says, living
on this street, all these years, she says,
I've been dying to touch the water out there,
all these years, she says,
my back to the wall.

The cool air is so deep inside her
the gentle breeze
never reached her heart, or the porch,
even to blow a kiss across the street,
even to make a prayer in someone's name.

LIFTING THE HORIZON

She could not look at her mother's face
as it fell away. With raised and praying arms
she waited for the D train
to Prospect Park. She sat by herself
waiting for the arrival, for some destination,
and then her long walk. In metaphor
she could always understand what was meant
but now inside her brain it felt
like fires were climbing over each other
up the mountain and the trees were exploding.
It was one fire storm after another. She thought
of going to a movie, middle of the day.
She watched the trucks and people moving
in the mirror of a window. This train
she thought, is bound for glory. Or, if not
the train, at least she would see that her mother
believed in the cemetery of life. Somewhere
in the Park, walking toward home according to plan,
she would slip her hands under the horizon, and lift
and there would be so much light.

AND SO IT GOES

These sidewalk preachers remind me of men in a car who pull up to a woman and wolf-whistle and scream and bark and pound on the car doors. What do they think? That the woman will swoon, overcome with love?

- Luis Alberto Urrea

THE FIRST POEM

Every poem is written
in the shadow of death
missing the local laughter
we've seen in other
lives. The guest poet
was introduced as
Jane Kenyon's widower
just like the rest of us!

I.

UP AND BACK, INTO THE AIR

THE BLACK SEA

It looked blue to me
but as you all know
I have been wrong
before. No one I
talked to on the
Turkish coast could
give an explanation
for the name. It seems
one of those mysteries
we face when we are
the least bit alert
or very lost. When climbing
out of our painful
selves we often will
attempt a bargain, make
a deal between where
we have been and what
we can't quite see
ahead. In this case
trying to bluff is very
dangerous. None of us
really has what some
call a "poker face."
We give it dead away.
Just go the way of the
Prophet named Oti
(we think), and this wisdom:
"Poetry is like driving a truck
5,000 miles to a town
worse than yours."

SMALL WHITE WOMAN

You are a small white woman.
You toss yourself out the door.
I just glanced out my study
Window and saw a young man
Riding a unicycle carrying
Something under each
Arm, something like framed
Paintings or pieces of cardboard.
I glance out the window now
And he is empty handed and
Walking the unicycle up the street,
North this time, instead of south.
The direction he is going won't
Help him, it is 100 degrees
North two blocks, south two
Blocks. Your child should learn
Maps – we are all geographically
Challenged. Once you are outside
The door in your small
White woman dress where
Will you go? You could come here
But my AC is broken,
As is most everything else.

VIOLIN

I'm sorry that our
Discussion about
Your violin-making
Was interrupted.
I remember you said
Ten so far and it
Started as a hobby.
Then we both got
Distracted as others
Welcomed us to
Our destination, the Jacobean
Era, James I, 1603-
1625. Some in the know
Claim it as the high point
Of English drama with
Shakespeare, Donne, and
The King James Bible. But who
Is making the violins with
All of this drama?
Who is conquering who and sending
Them into slavery or the
Drama of the stage. I
Can't remember, were they all
Men or all women dancing
And acting, reciting the words
Of the drama Kings? It is all
So dangerous as one

Person hearing or making
It up – something you said against the King –
Could send you straight to the Tower,
Your candy-apple violin bleeding.

THE GENIUS COMES HOME

How do you keep
all of that information
in your head?
You remind me of
a small quiet
wisp of a
cloud that in
a few seconds
explodes into a
storm-filled rush
of hail and wind
five miles in
the sky. Then
like the storm
you act on your
natural instinct
and come crashing down
on all of us
within your reach.

HELADO MAN

The helado man pedals his bike with the cold box
fastened to the front. He wears a cowboy hat and sounds
a very quiet bell as he comes down my street. A larger
"good humor" ice cream van plays the universal and
obnoxious tune to warn the neighborhood. The dogs,
usually behind fences, go crazy at the van like it's an intruder
or a police car. The helado man goes quietly down
the street and around the block without a sale. Then
on Wednesday evenings and Sunday afternoons I see him
across the street, very happy, with his bike and ice cream box
fastened to the front, as he anticipates the mass exodus of
worshippers, especially children, at El Templo de Nueva Vida.
Everyone crowds around him like he was a long-awaited
abuelo!! The "good humor" man misses the new life by a mile.

TORNADO ALLEY

Maybe more storms across
The Central Plains over the
Next few days, possible
Tornadic activity. We have
No shelter. Hail comes hard
And destroys the flowers.
Then heavy rain flooding
Our escape and in the rain
Cloud is the swirling storm
We know so well. No shelter,
No radio that works, can't
Hear the sirens. Oh, the sirens
Singing out to us some fake
Lyric of safety and pleasured
Relief. But we can't hear them.
We only see the stripped and
Tortured trees, piles of brick
And splinters of wood. There is
Just too much damage
To rebuild this life.
Require the shelters and save
The sirens for our dreams.

ANIMAL

Sometimes I don't know
How to say words you

Will understand. My fault,
Not yours. My anger, not yours.

So when I throw this vase
Against the wall it is only

Because I don't have a job,
Mostly it is the fault of my

Speaking dis-a-bil-i-ty.
Some people say, what was that?

I say, what was what?
They say, that strange sound.

I say, I didn't hear anything.
They say, it was like an animal.

I say, I don't have any
Animals in my house. They say,

I heard something loud, from the
Deep throat. I say, I don't watch

Those movies, (got to get them
Off track!), "them" is you.

You have always had the wrong
Idea about me. I will hang (up) now.

ZADIE CREEK

--*"…and after a time I did not
feel the need for complete answers,…"*
-Lydia Davis

Like this creek, no complete answers.
Who was Zadie? Was she kind, abused,
stumble across or into this water, brown
and quiet, slow moving after her labor
birthing another mystery? What kind
of name is Zadie? Did she have long
hair, short, what color? Depending on
who's doing the talking, said the police
officer, the dispute was over a girl or
a dice game. "Not sure we will ever
know the truth." This is all for
a book I'm writing of non-fiction.
When someone asks me, Is it all true?
I say, True enough! (David Sedaris, paraphrased)

SLIP OF THE EAR

We went shopping
for mothballs
but came home
with a mattress.
There are those
times of durable
space between
sounds that
make for
noble actions.
Bless my soul,
the beggar said,
bless my eager soul.

CAUGHT IN THE ACT

You have this need to
Spread things around
On the table, adjusting
The scissors, prints
From Japan, endless small
Round pieces of paper from
The paper punch used
For measuring the state
Of mind you confess to
Like or pretend to translate
Into zero porn. Unrolling
The scroll you say is
Abusive to twenty centuries
Of linguistic kinetics
Back to the table
You make the music
With your hand as you
Place the legal document
In front of me
Keeping the children for
Yourself, leaving me out,
I sign on the line,
And my voice is a
Criminal act with
Sentencing to follow.

THE OTHER WOMAN

You would be hard to explain.
You come in and stand, walk around,
in and out the door. You go to the
playground.

Be careful. Watch your step. You go to the swing.
Up and back, into the air. You try to fly out of the way.

AS I GROW OLDER

I want fifteen (for now) important items
tended to in a timely manner:

Trim my toe nails
Trim my finger nails
Trim nose and ear hairs
Make sure my socks are clean
And my underwear, especially my underwear
And my glasses
I want my hair cut handsomely short and neat
like my scotch
I want my children, grand children and
great grand children to know I
am alive until I am not
Find the damn democrats some GUTS
Somewhere
Ask Cora to explain "SELF AS SOULMATE"
Treat every faith and non-faith
community carefully, we are
all terribly wounded
I am a "veteran of the cross" so see
if some money can come of it
When I stop laughing
someone pick up where I left off
Do you have any questions?

SAINTHOOD

Many in this dusty crowd
are calling for me to replace
St. Francis, it just seems that all
the animals love me and want to flock
around me wherever I am.
(Actually I keep spending a lot of money
 on bird feed so I am also building their
 dependence!)
So all this animal love isn't true anyway.
Take those loud dogs down
the street. If I would get
too close to the very low
wrought iron fence that brown
and black mongrel would have
my shoulder for lunch. Those
who see me as at least almost
equal to St. Francis are kind
and generous to mention it
and even thoughtful enough
to write the Pope. But my own desire
is to be seen more as St. Anthony. I was
reminded of this today when, Koldo, our
neighbor's one-year old boy, walked up to me
and held up his arms, he wanted me to hold him.
You see – Anthony is the only Saint ever
imaged holding the Christ Child.
Why is that? He is also the patron
Saint of the lost.

WINTERESS

The forsythia is struggling during
This last week of March. Perhaps it is
One of those specialists
In managing pain.
I am not one of them.
Not yet.
But with the help
Of the dark
Brown winteress
And a friendlier
Climate, both the forsythia
And I
Will thrive.

SPRINGTIME

I am urged to
"sleep like a baby"
but most of the babies
I've known in my life
slept like crap. The
refugees are now caught
along the border. They
cannot officially register
in the new country as
they are fleeing their own.
It is winter in these
mountains, springtime
in the meadows. Those
on the run need
so much and I stay
awake thinking about it.
But I think about
other things. How the
body can sabotage it's
own health, get back at
the emotional warfare it
has waged for decades.
Then again I see white
United Nations tents
in the dark snow,
mud, as ragged and hungry
freedom fighters track down

and kill the woman and baby
in a nightmare fight
like dogs over entrails
in this particular way.

FRAGRANCE

You remember that guy
whose mom gives
him shots in
embarrassing places?
She is the nurse,
a nice person.
He is older now by the day
but she helps make the
office visits easier. That sounds
like an old man basking
in flirtatious conversation,
smiles all around, unbuckling
his belt so she can get
the Demerol in his
hip. But it is not like that.
You may believe this or not
but the doctor event is
eased by friendship
and similar left-wing
political views. She wants
to hear about Bosnia,
the Middle East,
Gaza. No one is going to jump
into bed, no one. And I
disagree with my friend who says
we spend our lives
like dogs going around sniffing
each others' tails looking for
someone else, some new fragrance.

NAILS

Weren't we all like that?
Inherently and obviously
selfish -------
I told them my nails
just got done
it's too hard
to take off
and I wear gloves
I can't get them off
Save those nails, I say,
weren't we all like that?
Inherent and obvious
for all you've put into them,
save those nails,
selfless, I say.

MANOR CARE

It goes with the job,
Knowing the exit
Codes for all the nursing
Homes in town.
At my age
Setting off the alarm
At the door, just a few
Steps from my Honda,
Will mean being led
Kindly back
To some soft chair
In the reading
Lounge or to the
Recreation room
For the regular Bingo
Hour sponsored by God
Only knows whose
Best intentions. Then I drop
The book I'm reading
In the lounge,
Can't see the letters
And numbers on
My Bingo card. I sit
In my room, nothing
On the walls except brown
Paint. Through my window
I see lots of Hondas,
Any one of them
Could be mine.

JACK

The drought could continue for several years.
By then the reservoir that gives us most
of our water would dry up. Instead of
boats and other water sports we would
haul out our four-wheelers and moto-cross
bikes into a dry "sports world" for
our fun. You wanted to have a son
and name him Jack. This poem
will continue with even more intimate
details or, instead, just dry up for lack
of spring-fed fresh kisses. We are left
with the memory of water's drowning wave.

TODAY WITH THE DOG

Today with the dog walking
by the river, cold aching
in the legs. How did it
get this way so soon?
What a stupid question!
I know it was not an
overnight process. I can
tell you very specific times when
life was as unbearable
as it is for anyone and
definitely not as bad as
most men my age around
the world. In fact, I am
lucky to have this river,
a dog walking along covering
twenty times the territory
I am covering and damned lucky
to ache with the freeze of life.

WE WANT TO BE BETTER OFF

Those you see on the screen
are the lucky ones, they
at least have some debris
to work with. Splinters of
two by fours, broken
PVC pipe, various sheets
of plywood for a roof.
Those you don't see
on the screen are the unlucky
ones. They are under the mud,
their gravesites now the foundation
for this new village. No one
wants to talk to us, standing
as we are on their buried
families. [Sorry it has been
so long in this empty search] You,
he said, are not helping with your
words, microphones, and cameras.
We want to be better off.
Find your own red mud-slide
then try being photogenic.

ALMENA, NORTON COUNTY

My mother replied
that it was palsy
as she trembled in
cutting the meatloaf.
So are we all left
with that kind of
nerve which usually
means courage or
some nasty back talk?
She had a December
death and burial. You can
drive northwest from here
to Mt. Hope, looking over
the Prairie Dog valley,
to see the site for
yourself. No sign of palsy
or any kind of nerve.

II.

O TASTE AND DREAM

CORE WORK

My daughter instructs me
To sit on the large blue ball,
The size of an ottoman or hassock
But I am reminded of a distant Balkan
History lesson. She gets my attention,
Dad! You need to balance on the ball,
Both feet flat on the floor. I can't balance
On the ball as I am sure
She can see. Ok, put the ball up against the wall
First. Now, take a dumbbell, she looks at me with
A long pause, in each hand, alternate lifts, slowly,
Breathing in and out, in and out,
Slowly. But I have moved from the Balkans
To her wedding in a couple of weeks, walking
Her down the aisle, officiating at the service,
Kissing my daughter the bride
With my back hard against the wall to keep from falling.

WOLFGANG

-January 27

He wrote his first opera
at age eleven. What did
it get him? A handful of fire.
A middle class Vienna burial.

Then he and I worked together
to find a cure. He wanted to bring
a new composure to his life, turning
down even a requiem for himself.

Our plan was to complete a lyric
or libretto to win over a queen.
This would be the cure for all fear
of darkness, but deadly cold followed us.
Evitable
side step out of danger
move your junk down the alley

there is so much to avoid
like the taste of some
lover across the ocean through
straw and wine and apples

this life is so full now
of escape and rivers
you hoped would be the
passport to other phone

calls but they turn
out only to
be your sad

and long path
to the evitable

OPPOSITIONAL RESPONSE

You say you will but you don't.
All your life you have worked your
muscles against the prevailing
current, set sail for an island
you could not reach with the usual
breeze. Bring the cape to me,
you said, then I'll set it to storm.
You have a natural way of doing
the opposite as you pull your enjoyment
keeping us all guessing as to what
is next. Whatever is the accepted
truth you claim as betrayal and
anytime you are offered some treatment
(like talking to Luisa, 5 years old, grand
daughter, and daughter of Joel and Tracy)
for your condition you run the
other direction. O taste and dream
you warn all of us. Your sacred
writings rely on asymmetric,
through-the-back-door, soft-core
porn responding to the swarm of waves
as they come in across the sun
making "time" your child to raise with
love and the "fisted minds" of Ephesians.

DECEMBER IN KANSAS

Thank you for the phone call.
I just finished putting three
exams together to give
tomorrow. I walked the dog
in the near dark over
by the river. The wind
was cold, from the north,
stinging my face. It felt
like a soft touch, advent, waiting
for a new skin, born,
reminding me of Montana,
of myself, of a new world caressed
and cradled in the warm fur
that carries our lives away.

SOLITARY CONFINEMENT

You don't have to do what they say.
Find your own way through the
demands and expectations of every
phone call or sexy move. The
daylight is more convenient for those of
you who wish a more visible truth. During
the dark you can solve or disrupt
the life of anyone's dreams. You can
offer this access to art that most
will not feel but only disregard.
Or you can feed on the brain-cleansing
spices that make memory more of a clear
domain rich in life experience, and
beach memories and full pages of solitary
confinement. You will find that even
when the war inside you breaks loose
your truth will be a casualty soon,
if not the first. Then you will seek
some negotiation for peace, for an end
to unquiet losses, something to make you smile.

LEARNING ENGLISH DURING A WAR

I'm afraid of going into
the opaque places,
there would be no
adjacent safe homes.
I am strengthened
by the courage of my
children as I have
dialogues at last
for a while. Now
I must obey this
mutual cease-fire.

SOMALI PIRATES NOW FACING BOREDOM

God is not so great! Not a ship in sight.
And all these hostages
to feed. And our wives.
I can't even get in my boat
to take a swing
at the sea. No fuel.
And no ammunition – spent it all
stupidly shooting in the air
at weddings and other parties.
From now on all celebrations
are banned!
Where's the rice and coffee?
The cigarettes? My deck
of cards?

You can tell everyone
is getting edgy. Just to glance
at a lone 30-footer with
those clean white sails
spreading wide with invitation.
A beauty like that would
lift our spirits high. Speaking of wives,
where are they?

IN THE PARK

In the park with the leaves,
she walked a step behind him
with her hand gently
resting on his left shoulder
as they walked. They already
understood what took me
most of a lifetime to figure out.
They knew we all share
this planet like a vast
costume party, that some
of us are dressed as angels,
others as monsters. They
somehow knew that the blood in our
violent dreams is a sign
of life, and the pain of giving
away half - or more - of
your heart to another means
that only foreigners or someone's
god can help us now.
Through my cataract eyes
it was obvious, but blurred.
They knew in their walk in the park
with the leaves, they knew,
so much that I had long forgotten.

GRAPSKA

BOSNA i HERCEGOVINA

Near Grapska is an orchard.
I've never seen it, though some
of my trees are there. The photo
shows rolling hills with trees
unlike the Flint Hills
of Kansas. Also in the photo
is the real owner of the land
trying to make it beyond
survival of war, landmines
and no money. He is holding
the saplings of peach, pear
and apple. He cradles them
like a new born,
a bundle with roots
to join the dead and be raised again
as a peaceful lion, raging lamb.

MANY THANKS (STANDING OVATION)

This was easily my best performance
fooling even the harsh critics of the
Times and The New Yorker. The rabbit's

timing was impeccable appearing from
the hat exactly on cue. The girl (young
woman) was cut in half, thirds, and then

made it out alive, in one piece. Coins
appeared everywhere, in shoes, behind ears,
falling from the ceiling. People went mad.

I was making miracles, turning peaceful
people into my soldiers. Just a few words
like: "You are getting sleepy..." and they were

molded before my very eyes. There was no
resistance. I could believe in them to help with
the war effort, lose all inhibitions. They went mad.

ASSISTED LIVING

I remember the stairs.
The wood without railings
years and years of laundry
and checking the furnace
but I don't know you.

There was a huge sky
with millions of stars
touching my face like
a gentle straight drop
of snow. You have a kind voice.

I can see the birds
out a large window.
They are at a feeder
I hung from a branch.
I know you've been here before.

Could you put the suitcase
by the door, the blanket over my
shoulders before you leave?
It makes me feel adored.
Thank you. I'm going home tomorrow.

SYNCOPATION

We all roll around
in the belly of the beast,
burn the music and
the poet as stakeholder
running her fingers along
the ribs of your rough
ground, pop the match
for your Lucky Strike
in plain sight of all
this open and rolling grass,
and a loose syncopation
brought on by
the instant change
of your heart's weather
and the cold and the
word sliced by the other.

DOGS

All of these dogs
were bouncing and
playing on the tracks.
Trains came often and I
was trying to warn
the dogs that their
lives were in danger,
a horrible death could
happen if they
didn't stop messing
around on the tracks.
They would not listen.
They were having so
much fun. I was
dying with fear and
the image of the remains
when Union Pacific,
or was it the Rock Island,
came through. I was just
a young boy but I
was trying to be a man.
That's what I could not
convince the dogs of, that
I was a man. I am still
working at it, still calling
the dogs away from the
tracks, the noise of
so many trains keeping
me awake all night. I was
this close to being a man.

THE SKELETON BUS

You have brushed your hair,
put on your face,
dressed in extra large
clothes looking
beautiful and
lethal. Having trained
for this you go
through the check
point without fuss
and walk past
shops and cafés
toward the bus
stop. Number 42
comes along on time,
packed with all
these people. You
put on your face,
just to take it off.

THE REPENTANCE DOOR

-Holy Kaaba, Mecca

On the 18th floor lives a beautiful woman.
That's all I need or want to say. Except
that she is married, has two kids, and
a nice smile, which I mentioned to her
with and without objectivity. I believe
in affirmation and that none of us in this world
receives enough. We spend so much time, like lice,
crawling into the seams of other people's skin and
clothing, burrowing deep to make ourselves
invisible but cause great irritation and pain. We do our best
not to be discovered, to avoid being plucked out
of our cozy rash. There are other peaceable
lives we could live. There are doors we could
pass through on a regular basis to create a
thoughtful and kind apartment building. We
could share each other's holidays, respect privacy,
shred the money, water all the plants, give
a generous gift. This entire building could be a model
community of everything good and healthy, even
have a lavish roof-top garden of flowers for love
and vegetables for slow meals shared on beautiful
Turkish carpets spread out under the stars. We could
tumble around on the wool, drink strong coffee, hold the sleepy
children in our arms. Comfort is also something we all need.
We are desperate for kindness and caress. Let's drive the lice
from our lives and the pain will transform into

energy for walking miles across mountains and prairies,
rush through airports, catch the right bus to arrive
at the repentance door. Dare to enter, for it is nothing after
all we have gone through these past 10,000 years.

JACK MORGAN

The oceans have a long memory.
I kiss my hands and taste the salt.
It is a way of showing respect,
a greeting, a goodbye. Two good
friends died in the past couple
of weeks. I know it happens. I've
done the funerals, been at the death
beds, helped the pale morticians carry
the body around tight corners out
of sight of the family. I've closed
the eyes staring at dead ceilings,
helped the fainting women who come up to the
open coffin to see their cousin,
niece, son, with bullet-shattered reconstructed faces
no one really recognizes. We all scream
louder than the grieving choir while Jack,
at the organ, keeps us moving past all
the dead ones, playing, "Precious Lord, take my hand."

HEAT

Thinking of you on the train
Back from Lyon – long story –
And how your life
Is up for grabs, in the balance,
Dealing love and sadness
Like a hand in poker, not
Hearts. Adding my life to
Yours plants some beauty
Along the tracks. I believe
All the things you say I am.
Travel safely to the unspeakable
105. Glad you have
A river to walk.

THE COMPLETE POEMS OF DEBBIE OCEAN

It is now the calm after the storm.

I want another word for hope, another language.

Are you in the mood for ultimate Karaoke?

Right now I have more children than problems.

Even full rhyme, like crime, doesn't pay.

I have a friend dying tonight in Bethlehem.

What 15th century Italian tried to make you American?

Put people with dogs in Room 407.

There's been another death in the community.

Beauty hurts, but do you know that much about pain?

You lived for two years in a tool shed.

Foot-washing on Maundy Thursday, not my thing.

How much healing can a person take?

I have an appointment with Mohammed at 10 this morning.

Dry air is the singer's enemy, but not the only one.

50 N. PROFESSOR ST.

He meant to find lodging for himself,
a place that would be bright and
warmer than outside. Grey skin-clouds
surrounded his bones and ached for
the break-up of water and sky. Then
it became a nightmare of horses melting
in the mud trying to pull away as they
dissolved in the wallow of
slow exhaustion. There was nothing
he could do except wake up but he was
trapped in the bodies of the horses stripped
of muscle, changed to slop, sliding
into the chamber of breathing only
out, never in, always out, never
to regain the pulse of a life with
the good strength and form he once
had as a young man, like the winning
quarter-horse, spitting blood.

AQUIFER

Like most underground water supplies
you are being depleted. You have
to share in so many directions

mostly sold below market, mostly sad.
Restoration to better than normal
will take years, if ever. The art

of caring for resources is nearly
forgotten. It is a cycle of love
and death that barely wakes you up

even on a morning with sweet water
brought to you, a fresh well discovered,
still just so overwhelming, so close to empty.

PROSPERITY PREACHER

Her face was as long
As 17th Street. No place

To sit down
Or grab ass

And no energy
For either. Just

Standing. Someone
Will come along

With an offer
Of good juice,

A drink of the real
Stuff, around

Your arms, in
And between all

That is lonely
Aching for the silent Jesus prayer

And yet warm and smooth enough
For a full-throated amen.

NOT EVEN IN A BLUE MOON

There are continents
looking for a sign
of faithfulness
to the end.
And there is you.
The walk you promised
yourself along the edge
of one land mass
also brings you close
to your voyage. My
adventure will be to sit
on this front porch
and taste the passion
of the thunderstorm
rolling across the prairie
from the west,
from all we never touched.

THE OAK

The oak tree
naked from the moths

of winter
goes for a walk.

You work at your
desk, morning

writing. Love in
the midst, the mist

but still scared of
the wide open places.

PLANTING

The instructions say:
Use adequate water.
What does that mean?
What is adequate?
Place already dead-looking roots
In adequate mix
Of sandy and low Ph
Soil. Place pine mulch,
An adequate amount,
Around the roots for a
Good start for growing
Toward the sun, full sun!
Moisture should go down
Six inches into the soil,
Do not soak, keep the roots
From rotting to death. It's an
Adequate life. Not too much
Of this or that. Not too little
Of everything else.
Dirt, peat moss, mulch,
Manure, sand, adequate water.
Like the instructions tell us
On the package
In several languages,
Don't overdo it.

NOMADIC

That label does not mean
you are without a home.
It means, if someone gives
you some frequent flier
miles, you take them
gratefully, and plan
a journey away from
the sheep and goats
you have to care for
every day. Hopefully,
an ocean away from
the drudgery of finding
enough green pasture for
those creatures making
daily demands…and
water that they can
drink but you cannot.
They survive on the barest
essentials but it all leaves
you exhausted where even
home is not a comforting
stable. It's complicated
territory, even with its
beauty, so move on
for a while, make good
use of the gift of miles
so nomadic becomes another
word for the future of love.

III.

"HORSE" IS HEROIN

RULES OF WAR

The law says all
invaders must show
some respect for the
indigenous residents.
But invaders don't
do what they are told,
they conquer, plunder,
ravage. Read your
history books. Watch
your neighbors. Be ware
of those for whom
you have most opened
up your beautiful heart.

DRIFTING

I am waiting.
As a kid I waited
for darkness with fear
and needed a nightlight.
Then years later, recovering
from cancer, I needed
at least to see the streetlight,
so the dark was not total
and I could wake up at 3 a.m.
to reassurance. Now
I am back to waiting for
the dark but as
comfort, as a way to stop
the bombardment of feelings
that terrorize during daylight.
Closing my eyes, the fear
now is wakefulness
the inability to shut
it all down even for
a while, in the bliss
of full sleep. And
I wait for that time
when I can drift
toward the dark shore
that is not a raft.

THE GAZA BALLOON

It's a breakdown
Kind of day. One
For announcing a
Hunger strike or
A march for peace.
The rocks will always
Be here, they will
Outlive the fancy
Weapons. We will
Keep throwing the rocks
Until we are all
Arrested or the other side
Comes to a fair
Agreement. I know
You like flowers and
You accept them with
Such joy and grace.
You embrace them
And it feels like me
In your arms. We are
Watched from the sky
By the surveillance
Balloon, as we are
Arm in arm. Even
With the disengagement
Letter between us
The border guards

Allow us a brief
Touch, hand to hand,
Better the tears than blood.
Looking for your dream home
you glance through the morning paper
to find the "Home and Garden" section.
You really think it will be there.
Must have the right lawn, bay window,
red brick of your childhood. You
remember the nights
when you would let
the boys touch you, and
you still want that kind of red
brick. You went home wondering
why it felt good and who would
find out. So now a deep green
lawn seems right, filled with
new possibilities. Not love exactly,
not love at all, never love. But a
near notion of what it might be like
to experience a breakthrough, a "what now,"
a crossroads. None of these homes – or gardens –
give you a sense of solution, of
conviction, and now it is dark,
time for sleep, time to hide.

IF YOU TAKE

If you take the waters
From each sea
And wash with the salt
And the fish, what will
Happen? If you take your
Life and come up with
Unexplained disasters and joy,
What has happened?
In this world the love we
Live with moves around
And through us bringing
What we renounce and
Our alone loneness. These
Lines move through
And around gender and
Touch, withheld and
Only with…held. Soon
All will fall inward and we
Lose or gain what someone
Else wants. You can take
The waters, the salt, the fish
And let them caress you
And you will be seen as strange.

MAN DISGUISED

"Man disguised as tree
Robs bank..." Was he
Deciduous? Or Evergreen?
Flowering? Needled?
We'll never really know.
There are so many places
He could hide. How do we
Know the tree was a man and
Not a woman? Facts are
Hard to come by and often
Only hide the truth. Even
In the natural world of
Weather and wind and fire,
Reality is only as good as
The heart that floods to
Overwhelming. Imagine the
Police artist trying to render
A sketch of the true criminal?

e

I went late to check my Post Office box,
Startled by a cough, I turned to see
The lady, sitting, staring straight ahead
As if she saw something bearing down
On her. Maybe it was her work, limited now
To the PO lobby, her years, and
Unable to anymore sing about guarantees she handed
Out like her tongue on good nights. I had trouble
With my key, distracted by the old lady, was this
A set up? I looked around, be alert stupid, but for
The grace of god, you could be her, staring at some
Body bearing down on you, at a time
When even your good work qualified
And your nights came with pay and benefits.

VALENTINE'S DAY

The skeletons in your closet began
To rattle, whispering to each other, even
Competing for the most chaos
They could cause you. You woke up
At 3 a.m. and watched the snow
Falling with such innocence.
You tried to see over the rooftops to the end.
Do you want a dozen roses or the much cheaper
Grocery store minuet bouquet? Remember
All the love that has passed away?

THE ZOO

There was no hiding place as they bombed our books.

Then destroyed the U.N. building storing our food.

Then the hospitals were hit with U.S.-made rockets.

My uncle, my mother, father, our home are all blood-
stained rocks.

And my Gaza Zoo, with the terrified lions freed by the
shelling of their cage.

Finally, they were locked in some bathroom to keep them
safe.

Those who survived in the zoo ate those who did not.

BIRTHDAY

my waistline don't call
for a cake. maybe oreos
but only a couple because
my hips are the salvation
of the world like the left side
of the door that had a
sign reading, "use other door,"
because my ecstatic breathing
could rip you off your
hinges. what you might call
a perfect storm in my bed
i call too small to make
a wave or a tree to sway.

THE LIQ

Stop at the drive thru beer store
I need a 16 oz. cool for my good son
I called today and found my
Food stamps $200 for the month
For the seven of us   everything
Costs so much   I can't breathe
Air is too expensive

HOW DO YOU GET THE WHOLE WORLD

to yourself?
Find the weeping
love grass
hold it close
taste it down
to the deepest
root.

PUDDLED FABRIC

Try another fortune cookie,
Something simple like
You will soon meet
A new friend,
Or you are close to
A wonderful surprise.
Were we suppose to
Get together soon
And I forgot? You never
Call when it's the right
Time, first things last,
Right? It's a dance
Of follow and
Never lead
During this spring
Snow. Close the door,
Leave the puddle
Purple fabric on the
Floor as a clue.

"which keeps faith nimble"
Emily D.

the internet weights 2 oz.
like a strawberry, like a day
we've never seen
before
learning each other's
moves for the fascination
of it, o girl,
La Santa Cecelia,
patron saint of our songs,

"which keeps faith nimble"
cannot remember rain
but is so full after
the pre-nuptial dinner,
o girl, let justice roll
down your blouse like waters
and sing the saints up to the rafters,
call them crazy
but I'm not biting this time.

NO PLACE LIKE HOME

I live in
Kansas because
of the breeze
off the ocean.

Just like I live
in Gaza because
of the fireworks
every 2 or 3 days.

UNCLE HORSE

It's the shade
of morning and drifting
cool along the air
the ancient dress lifted
to the ankle. Then head
over heals the terror
remembered all night
when those horse muscles
worked and worked to finally
break open the stall.

MOONSHINE

He's been around
since Moses was
a baby.   Fixing
up 300 proof
for neighbors
and family.
He had the tasters
blind-folded
then carried them
out when they
were finished.
You think that's
just a story? I could
drag these all over
Oklahoma, my
blind eyes.

LEARNING ITALIAN FOR MY CAPTAIN

I learned my dread from the wet mouth.
Soon the children's story will belong to the soldier.
Starve for a week, no water for days, hair full of fist.
Night is misunderstood as an epic opera in every language.
It's been a lifetime of irony, nothing I see is as it seems.

PSALM 23

It means I don't
have to keep running
scared all the time.

A STUDENT OF SEPARATION

In the darkness
You have a heart
Attack of the brain.
You are one step
Away from your
Epitaph, accepting
Your ailment
As an assignment.
You don't mind
Coming home alone,
One light left on,
A very sick
And old dog in her bed
Living on liquid
Food. You quickly pour
Yourself a glass
Of wine. You think:
What's in it
For me? You're at the top
Of your class.

AND SO IT GOES

My face is not as fat
as it looks in
this mirror. It's amazing…
her mood swings could rival a
hurricane in the gulf. Battering me
all over the place…anyway, I'm off
to take the dogs for a walk which I haven't done
in forever since I've been ill…just managing
to keep grass to a manageable level and plants
alive in this heat—and feeding the kids—gotta
feed the little buggers, too. Someday I will regret
my resentment during such a poignant time
as my children's youth, and I wish it would
hurry up and come…see, regret and resentment could
arm wrestle and resentment can't keep up with
the facts, so regret would win. Also, as you know,
responsible parents blame themselves. Irresponsible
parents always seem to find an out…
and so it goes.

The Comedic Applicant

Part 1: Peeling the Orange

…we promise each other future celebrations

−Audre Lorde

The fiesta is a revolution in the most literal sense of the word.

−Octavio Paz

Instructions

May I peel this orange for you?
And just for your information
our snacks today are goldfish
crackers and pretzels. I will help you
in any way I can. We want you
to be comfortable for the entire
duration. If you need oxygen
please watch me as I show you
the proper way. Put this behind
your head, this over your mouth,
and breath as if you were alone.
Please remember we can never
predict clear air turbulence.
If there is a drop in pressure
take care of yourself first,
then the children. Don't
interfere with navigation
by using your pain to make someone else
laugh. You may be able to turn back
but I cannot.

Making Love

When will you know
whether your lover
has moved life for you
like a mountain? Then you
will have to make some
gesture of remembrance
and get well enough to walk back
through the town where your lives
came together. There is a house
you will both recognize
even in the tangled light
of your passion. There will be
people who still recall the shadows
you left in the lives of their children.
It's an old story that even
those who live without electricity
still pass on to the next
generation. No one will learn
from it. They will only live to witness
lover after lover startled by car lights
in the darkness or the phone ringing
just as they are about
to hold each other.

Professor of Voice

He makes the human sound as if music was the last breath
any of us take. He is caught up in the importance of his
profession and his diaphragm. We listen to his lecture in
the twilight of the day, the sun calmly settling our fears of
the coming night, our souls dancing like fingers wasting time
on a desk, the quiet thumping barely heard by the voice at
the front of the room. Soon he will tell us about his life or a
    moment
when it changed forever, usually an obscure musical piece
    that took the
place of love or, somehow, brought love alive. He can almost
    sing
his way into your heart but there is always a kind of pity that
follows close behind him like a pet and makes most of us
    want to avoid
his eyes. There are always, though, one or two who suck in
    the pity
as if they were taking a gasp of drowning air. They are
    touched by his
tumbling story and and want to create more movements for
    him so his
vocalized loneliness will stand a chance in the world. It's not
    feeling sorry
for him but a desire to breathe again. We all have that desire,
    a mute
hope—that somewhere, in a glorious moment, in front of
    eighty thousand

cheering fans—we all will find a mode or chord or even a quarter of a note of breath that gives us the feeling that we have just escaped a raging and deadly army and found our own dry ground in the midst of the siren and the sea.

Small Town Forensics

The audience here always applauds
at the wrong time. They never
get it right. It's not a matter
of sophistication
but the kindness of neighbors. No one
wants to hurt another's
feelings. So if the music
stops only for a breath
we all think it's time
to show appreciation. The same
was true when your brother
was shot. The neighbors
came in before the body
was removed. They began to clean the kitchen
so you would not
have to see the blood.
The gun was handled by several
well-meaning men before it was sent
to the lab of state. Weeks went by.
No decision could be made
as to cause. The autopsy was
a joke. They never got it right
and so you go on with your life
because everyone has been so nice.

September 9, 1999

You go around to all the windows
opening the shades and trying to find
as much light as you can. You want
to clean house, listen to Sorrowful Songs
of Gorecki, fall in love with yourself
once more so you can survive the long drive
toward another family emergency. You then
cannot find your key to the sanctuary
which leaves you alone out of control,
in the cold, barely speaking the language.
You thought he died sometime in August
not September. Your father's voice is still
on your answering machine. What was
the question? You push the switch and his
words remind you to forget. You fly off to work
to take care of business, all those demands of
slaying all those dragons of evil.

Kansas Bumper and Body Parts

—words seen on the side of a large truck

One U.N. worker was attacked
by a mob, stabbed and killed. Otherwise
the elections were peaceful. This was the NPR report
on the local public radio station
here in Kansas. It came just as a truck
passed in front of my car
at the intersection. This large truck moved
quickly through the yellow light
with the momentum of dead weight
falling out of your arms.
The news continued . . .
a new month began as more invasions
and elections were held to try to pull
people together but seemed, according to all
accounts, to only sever relationships and spread
the blood around. AIDS deaths are reaching what they call
a "plateau." Lovers and younger are less protected.
What is it like to be a lover?
Is it carrying the dead weight
through the intersection, avoiding the mob,
red light, and believing that with just one death
the peace has not been broken?

Album of 400 Memories

Leafing through the catalog you say this photo album
would make a nice gift for someone. They could place their
    pictures
in the clear plastic holders, one behind the other, and when
they lift up the photo the other would appear. It is a
    convenient use
of space, an invention
made for profit and delight of memory
storage unlike any other method. at the touch of a finger
    the past
is instantly moved
and the viewer can smile, laugh, or remember
the sorrow many pictures, even in color,
capture. And if there are more than four hundred memories
there is always the heart to recall
the faces, the music, distant friends, the years
of growing and leaving and coming home. Then the explanation
    of who is who
and why. People are naturally curious about such things
    whether or not
they ask. So you order the album, and maybe a shower curtain,
or another basket for someone's wedding someday. We could
even use the space for pictures the album
would provide. Then with the touch of a finger
all the colors of the rainbow would appear
for nothing now is simple black and white.

Immigrants

I haven't seen the news today
have not heard about the two
hostages. There is more tea
in the kitchen but you have another language to learn
before you can stop. Your labor
is exhausting us. As angry
as you are why do you
sleep at all?
The mountains were surrounding our life.
the soul could not touch the snow
that buried this marriage. All that we
learned on this land will be a life-time.
and death just seems to go together.
O, beautiful mountains
we left behind to break
new sod dreams. No flowered meadow.
No clear stream.

Vesper, Kansas

I always have magic recipes.
I have been drawing you
to me and have your face
in my mind
forever. Now,
you take the last light
burning an orange
hole in the horizon
and hold it close
like you might
an old flame.

Like a Home

breathing stars
bright hair
bright life
so much nerve
on the question
of babies
and rocks
red as needles
the empty
pillow
named snow-
white

Blue Valley

Fatigue ambushed me. My guess
is that grief is somewhat like that.
Then we can move together across
the street and never be seen
because of the snow and all
that comes between us. You have always
asked for honesty and I was
never aware of fighting for words
but it has come to this last breath.

Carthage Still Exists

The dream is of your father
and the two of you dancing.
The music comes and goes
like the cold and hot
of the desert
or the beast and the beauty.
Just a few miles from Tunis
lies Carthage, still a city
with a street named Hannibal.
The elephants came this way
when trees were rooted
to the ground and the dream
of conquering the world
made love in your mind.
And you thought Carthage
was dead—you thought
the earth was covered
with sand and the dance
with your father would carry you
to all the water you could drink.

Scotland

Clouds tomorrow
certain as lovers
against the world.
There's a different light
here almost
a dance
or falling
toward a mirage.
A mirage. Is it all
crazier now
than ever?
When it seemed
right and calm?
We look at the castle,
the beach,
the North Sea–
bring a handful
of stones
for our home.
There is grass here
green as the other side.

Flying

You often see people embrace for the first time
and then for the last
at the same moment. It takes a certain
kind of breathing to live through
the fragments of life that make love
out of disintegration. Soon you
watch the crescent moon
out the window of the plane
as it makes a turn over the mountains
toward the stars that will guide
you into the night sky. You
can smile now
because the city is far below
and your work there
is done. The gift of being
a daughter, even abandoned,
has been received
and you can reach an
altitude that has nothing
to do with this plane or
the sky but only the limits
of your first-child obsession.

Palm Sunday

We ramble along
between joy and death
with a young boy's cough and cry
across the hall. The world today
does not have enough
space for departure
so we enter the city
of commotion not knowing
what all the quiet is about.
There could be a new attack
from a different angle
and we have no defense.
There is good reason to believe
we are outnumbered
and do not have
the weapons to strike back.
So many of our friends
and neighbors throw down their
blankets and outer garments,
tear branches and leaves from
the nearest trees to cover the road
into town, all for someone
who is human and confused.

River Blindness

Bookcases,
other furniture
that I discovered
in the disfigured dust.

Part 2: Going Through Moods

Surf Motel, Marysville, Kansas

Smoking or not? King or Queen? One night or more? I just
want to stay here forever along Highway 36 and watch
trucks from all walks of life downshift into the lower limit
of speed to keep awake to Colorado. I have abandoned
the interior of my natural sobriety and given up on
the church. Or did it give up on me? Only half
of this town's name is Mary. The other half has to do
with a place to live, a village, a home–a location to be
buried or scattered. I surf the television and am
reminded of war and eleven-year-old killers getting back
at classmates and teachers. Most of the shows are from
the past when I was a kid and they are now the popular
ones. But the past isn't always better and I find
myself fighting for some future that is more
promising than paralysis or free fall. I want to raise
my fist in the air like Nelson Mandela on the postcard on
my desk and proclaim freedom from perpetual reminders
of how easy it is to be tumbled around in the storm surf
we wait for most of our life–freedom to drown our
sunburned bodies or, with lungs aching, push off
the bottom sand with weak legs and break through
the surface for our saving breath, Will one key be enough?

The Eucharist

We have to understand why this wandering around the
streets is so touching. There is snow and ice which makes
each step something more than mere imagination. Why
do they call these buildings "skyscrapers" when there is
so muchsky above them, so much of what many would
call heaven? You hold your cup of coffee close to you
and pretend it is the finest brandy and we are making
conversation with diplomats from countries that have
proven how death is so much a part of life. Then you
speak to your own senator and test his knowledge of
compassion and streets. As an advocate you feel he does
not get it. You continue on and go out the door of your
imagination and it's something like Alice in Wonderland
because it feels like you are tumbling down a long
dirty tunnel with no way to stop. In the twisting and
turning it now begins to feel more like it would to spin
out of control in a crashing airliner with so many people
screaming and praying and holding their hands
and their babies. You are dropping out of heaven
and coming closer to the sky. The lights
of the city become your neighborhood and you are sick
from all that brandy, all that touching and churning,
all that you had imagined to be the truth. You hold
the cup closer and make conversation.

The Girl from Kosovo

There are those friends of mine for whom the writing
of a poem, or rather the composing of a poem
on a laptop computer or other electronic device
is pushing art into the unspeakable; it is dirty
like planting landmines at the high school.
But I am sitting here in the Dallas airport
having just swallowed a "solo pizza"
and a Diet Coke and I have this urge to write.
I don't want to dig down into my bag to find
my notebook even though I have two pens
in my shirt pocket. I am surrounded by the noise
of so many people I don't know and they are traveling,
like me, into the night to arrive
at destinations that may startle or elate.
Perhaps someone's laptop awaits them.
Is that too obvious a pun? You tell me
if you can. But first tell me why
the Kosovo teenaged girl on the radio
said: "I've seen so many beheaded bodies
and massacred three-year-olds that I am
just glad to be alive. It used to be unsafe
in the streets; now it is a danger to be home."
I don't think she cares if I write
on my computer here in the Dallas airport
thinking of her and the voice that dies away
like planes moving in the dark
away from the terminal.

National Baseball Congress

From the first base line you can see
40,000 foot high clouds in another state
where severe warnings have been issued.
It is 8:37 p.m. and still
90 degrees but a light breeze helps and watching
for foul balls hit in our direction is somehow
enjoyable. Where else could you see a team
from San Francisco and one from El Dorado
play baseball? Of course, another question is
why? And I suppose the answer could involve God
and pleasure but neither of these seem to work.
with high fly balls drifting toward the left field
fence, you think of some crazy details of
childhood. You didn't have to imagine monsters
because they came and sucked the life out of you
while little monsters laughed as they made
the circle around you smaller and smaller.
Finally, you feel like the baseball itself
with a small hard core, string wrapped together to cover
the tension and hold it in. The circle becomes complete
when you are tagged, as the players call it,
and find yourself the object of everyone's eyes
as you leave the circle, fly over the center field wall,
bounce across the pavement of a church
parking lot and come to rest so far away
not even God or pleasure will find you.

You Go Through These Moods

I've been buying flowers for myself
lately, You know I can be oblivious
to so many things around me. I know
it hurts people, But look at who
I am. Look at this freedom
glowing in my face. You reach
across the table and touch my cheek.
You could not help it, right? It felt
so warm and welcome, the invitation
was so natural. I want to be in a place
where the passing from one millennium
to the next comes as quietly
as watching a candle or
almost holding your hand.

The Ring

Your naked hands
are proud of you. They
want to show
the world how it feels
to begin a day without
attachments to fingers
or love lost, or details
of a life repeated
and repeated until
even you throw
those hands in the air
and surrender.

Light

Do you have matches behind your eyes?
Or a way to reach into your pocket
and pull out a spark of light that ignites the sky
just for fun? You seem like the kind of person
who would be able to do those tricks
and never miss a beat. Your paintings
do not scream at the viewer but they do ask
for more. They ask in a quiet way
like someone with desire
glancing across the room
into love's eyes–then
walking away
burning hope like a bridge
behind them.

Waiting for Storms: Newark Airport

In the boarding area the departure times are always changing. Tempers flare like danger signals on the highway. Police suddenly appear searching this area for fugitives from other flights. Standing at the urinal, another man speaks, as if to me, and I hear — "Is Lucy around? I need to talk to Lucy and have her make some airline changes for me"– he had a damn cell phone tucked under his chin. I washed my hands and looked up to find two police officers watching me, looking under the doors of stalls, waiting for storms to explode in their boring airport lives. Then Boston's Logan closes because of lightning. I continue my reading about new death squads in El Salvador. With half the population under 18 the homicides are against the children and gang members, who are children who may, or may not, have grown up. I remember that every two days a classroom of children dies by gunfire in the United States. People in other countries are afraid to come here. Maybe Boston will open up soon. Sunshine has just interrupted a good rain.

The Unquiet

–Tijuana, 1999

This early in the morning
beneath banana trees
your mind is quiet.
In the midst of two million
people and days
of moving dirt
and cement
by hand, wearing
a black
back brace
church bells ring–
welcome or come
and join us, or,
perhaps,
watch out
for Jesus
in the dust.

Blessed Sacrament

–Tijuana, 1999

You see the lightning from
the second storm. Even
as an arm baby
you cannot lift Jesus
because neither your
strength nor mine
can remove
–"los rostros de la violencia–
the face of violence.
You never
wear a watch,
always late,
always lost. You know
the streets
but not much about
where they will
lead you.

From Here

I fixed the two clocks in my office
so I could be on time or have time
for the next meeting or appointment
or session with the couple not willing
to ask forgiveness.

                They have become colder
in the past few weeks and that makes
me worry about my strategy
in working with their dreams
and visions for some kind of life
beyond grief and court settlement,
beyond love and losing half of all they own.

                Soon they will have to make
a decision
and now it is so quiet in this office I can hear the clocks
stealing more time from their lives
and mine. Who do they think they are?
That has been the question for months, if not years.

The Yellow Bed

"If Happiness is contagious,
You should be delighted."
–Continental Airlines paper napkin

At the grocery store
sometime in the
past few days
I bought a yellow
carnation. The woman
taking my money
the clerk
lifted the flower
by the stem
to smell the blossom
then set it down
never looking
at me
smiled in the distance
beyond the walls
of the store
even beyond this country
smiled gently
not at me
lifted the flower
to again smell
the blossom and smiled
far away
tasting someone's outdoor market.

The Souvenir from Where You Didn't Go

You didn't want to stay awake as you lift away
into sleep, into the tunnel, the turmoil, and you hear
    laughing
as you remember reading somewhere that only
the paranoid survive. You see in your dreams the
    buildings
where only soldiers are allowed with their official
documents, file folders with names blotted out.
You think about your definition of "terrorist."–Why
there is no news about what you know as truth
and blood and knives. Today fifteen people sang
    against war
that makes a refugee camp of the world. Why is there
    no memorial
to objectors? You ask so many questions and maybe
    that is what
keeps you surviving minute after minute when there
    is so little
nourishment let alone anything to sustain the smallest
    ounce of love.
Back to terror. You are losing ground because you
    have stood
up for yourself so many times and each occasion takes
that much more out of you. From the train you notice
    the dome
of the cathedral nearby. Soon even that sacred building
    will be destroyed

by "smart" bombs meant for dangerous targets, ones
    that could fight back if given a chance.
And these are not dreams now. It is all very real as it
    dawns on you
like the sun in the middle of a terrible rain storm.
    The hollow and honest eyes
behind barbed wire are like so many photographs,
    page after page
after page, and you know emotional generations have
    fallen
after so much work to rebuild. Can anyone tell? Or care?

Part 3: Solo

Another Poem with "Mercy" in the Title

I don't think there was much money in southwest Kansas
in 1921. And it
got much worse. The land covered
itself like a lonely quilted boy and the dust
swept in, not out. As a nine-year-old
boy it all seemed natural except the cattle
kept disappearing and all the adults
were angrier than usual. There was a rope
from the house to the barn. If you lost
your hold on the rope in the middle
of a dirt storm you might be found
just inches from home but also
only after the quilt was lifted. There is
a small booklet on the table
I notice as I am writing this poem.
It is just inches from my hand but it took
all this time to see it and read
the blue letters of the title: "Depression Hurts."

The Green Car

Behind me is a car, newer and larger than mine,
This car wants to get past me and after we make the turn
I look into my mirror out the back window and see
the car moving into the right lane. I am also moving
into the right lane. I am signaling my intentions. But it does
not matter. The green car is going to pass me on the right
so I, wisely in my opinion, move back to the left, again
signaling my intentions. I glance over and see the green car
speed along with more power than I have, or really want.
When the car is a safe distance ahead of me I move
to the right lane which is clear but I still
signal my intentions. I look forward in time to see
the green car pulling ahead into traffic and I can just
barely read what is called a "vanity license plate."
It says "MAPUTO." It is not a word one uses
in vain. It may be whispered to your lover at a delicate
time or as a code word for survival you hear
from the other side of the prison wall. Then you may
enter that city, choose your own commands,
and shout like a sea of love
moving into our nation's mouth free as fire,
burning for some future, or past attractive war.

Landing Lights

There must be some
proper distance
at which point the lights
shine in the darkness to signal
someone of our arrival. The rain
we did not even know
was falling threatens
to make a difficult
landing. An announcement
is made by someone
with authority in her
voice. Please take your seats
because even the pilot
is nervous. Of course, she does
not really say that. But with
all this rain and wind,
with dawn so far away,
it is clear that no light
will add much comfort
to the danger we approach.

Pushing Away from the Terminal

They might slow us down because
of the Kosovo crisis or the woman
using the "Airfone" in the seat behind me!
She is talking about what someone
can fix for dinner in her absence
and I see in the Washington Post
an editorial about handgun
legislation and, in another section,
the sensuality of Alvin Ailey's
dancers. As we begin our descent
I find it hard to listen to myself
and rush through this poem
I want to think more about the
sensuality of dancers. Instead,
low pressure in the sky outside
the plane reminds me of
the turbulence facing this whole
process of making it safely
to what is called home
and rain. But home has just
announced a holding pattern–
so, sensuality aside, the sky,
with all of these clouds,
beautiful yet keeping the pressure
on us, is so familiar. What makes
landing so important?

Solo

–For Jim King

The sky gets so intense
before a storm. At 3 a.m.
the sound of hail on the roof
reassured me
of the lost anger
found like a prisoner
escaping into the arms
of a swamp.
Tell me what the drums
meant to you. Just whisper
if you wish. I told you about
the closest thing to my
heart. Is that what
we all did? Your caring
profession is really
the oldest we know of
and the most deadly.

Interview with the Poet and the Lover

I've thought a lot about running away
but then I remember I would have
to take me along. I would have to answer
a lot of questions that I know have few
answers. I would have to study several maps
to figure out some possible destination and set aside
what to take which would be minimal. I travel
light at least on the outside. And you might
think–Oh, he has a mysterious and hermetic
inner life, a turmoil of sadness and loss
that are the real baggage–
You are right but our love for one another
drives me toward considering my life in another
light. Conversations we have bring some reality
back to my thinking. but that reality goes against
the rhythm of what is important. I can't say
much more because I may feel trapped into
speaking my own mind and everything right now
seems very explosive. I don't want anyone to get hurt.
I don't want people to read about my feelings.
I want everyone to just listen, keep watching from side
to side and to know that, when all is said and done,
I really like my smile.

The Warning

There is a high wind warning
for today
to let us know
of the danger possible
if we go further.
You have always been the one
to put up
a boundary. Your life
has always been
guarded.
But I have trouble
and push in spite
of warnings, bullets
spraying dust in front
of me. I still want
to go beyond it all
like some famous
fatal charge.

What More Could You Ask For?

The coffee was deep brown and the sugar
was sweet. This is some great way to start
the day. You managed to read through most of the paper
and did not have the day dreams that control
the light in your eyes. Downcast you have been
for so much of the time and looking for someone to force
happiness on you, but you have always successfully resisted.
Today someone opened a door for you and it was not
fear that allowed you to accept the gesture. The times
you have lived through are like warfare, undeclared, but
    bombs
and bullets are real as the front lines. You have screamed
and made the scars on your face with your own hands
but you have never lost your life. When you smile
we all have the hope of recovery and not just yours.
Having mowed the lawn today and smelled the freshly cut
    grass
you sit on the gray front porch proud to watch cars go by
and know this yard, yours, is ready for viewing. It is
such a beautiful night for baseball that you can't help
taking yourself to the game in town. You watch the perfect
    ball
bounce across the grass into a glove made of soft skin
and it feels almost like what you imagine as home.

Summary

It is meant to be this hot
at least through Monday.
Nothing will come to relieve
the high pressure
centered on this rock. You can
act in some exotic
or erotic way to make yourself
exciting in the heat of home
and fire. You might want to
approach Area 51
but you would then face armies
of questions and be detained
for days and nights. You have a special
night watch so you can
tell the time no matter what you are doing
or who you are with.
Find the cameras so you
can photograph your
tired legs and neck. You are so
lost now and in the midst
of the most restricted life
you can imagine.

A Postcard from Chicago

I hope you got to swim
with more dolphins
in Rhode Island,
terrific image. Some evil
virus has knocked me
out for a week. I went
to an exhibit on "The Healing
Arts of Tibet" and got laid
low by, no doubt, a roving demon
I'd sighted
at the exhibit. Karma.
Karma. Karma. And I
continue to love reading
church history (feminist authors)–
it makes much more sense
when one is feverish.

Eremos

*"Immediately afterward the Spirit drove him
out into the wilderness. . ."*
–Mark 1:12 (The Jerusalem Bible)

It is always Christmas
out here on the edge
where collateral damage
is not only explained
but presented
as a gift, Each time
there is a press conference
more innocents
are expected to die
because that is what happens
to the innocent–
by definition.
Is that so hard
to understand?
It is Christmas
in the wilderness
because there are angels
and there is fear.
Out here where there is nothing
your name is whispered
as listed among the living.

Forecast

This spring storm
coming down from
Dakota is filled
with snow making its way
into our lives
like the cold truth
that freezes
the heart.
We make the best
of the weather
as it changes
whatever it was
we said to each other,
the promise
of a warm front,
a light breeze,
sunlight. Promise
me one more time.

A Fantasy

Today is the day to conceive a baby with
a chance of being first when the calendar page
turns to 2000. You might think it is a clever
or cute way to start a poem but the one
for whom it is so important believes it is
written on the wall of the Superstition Mountains.
She views it as a lottery for the rest of her life. It is not silly
but she knows what you think as she
takes a short cut across a lush park with a name
neither she nor anyone else can pronounce. She moves
quickly as if someone is dying and has asked
for her. The pain often surprises her because it is so easy
to stuff it into a suitcase and run or the trunk of a car
like a body after a horrible murder and she has thought
of that too—homicide. A scoped rifle from the balcony
or a knife for a closer look at the pale face but none of it
makes any sense. Or all of it makes perfect sense.
It could even be laughable. Suicide has crossed
her lush mind but then she would lose it all. The options
are so few and tonight, finding the grace of a wide street
with so many people asking absolutely no questions,
making not the slightest demand, after all those years
of being moved around like a pawn, This is real hope,
out on the far edge, speechless, a heart of fool's gold,
and walking and walking and walking.

Part 4: Shalom

Lunch

Olives are forever.
I put them on my plate
and remember that not everything
lasts that long. There are
so many interruptions
in life, medical concerns,
deep and painful grief
that makes your heart
ache and feel it is ready
to explode. Then there is anger
like no one has ever seen before
and if it was to escape the skin
who knows what would happen.
But I want and declare
that the hope–so often invisible–
will also be made known.
I am going to fight
for what I usually
can't see, let alone describe.
Watch me–the whole world
can watch because I have
my hopes and dreams
and tears
and laughter and I will not hide.
What do you feel?

"She Won't Love You Any Less"

i liked the woman
on the phone
whom I knew
was my mother.
in person
it was something else.
was she beautiful?
i don't know
because we did not
see each other
long enough.
she liked to read,
had a favorite football
team and sometimes
remembered to send
a birthday card. born
in northwest kansas
she was quiet and kept
most everything
to herself. she liked
her grandkids, their mothers,
and usually asked about them.
but affection was as frightening
as making love. everything
always ended sadly
as she often told me.
the last thing she asked for

was a copy of
In Cold Blood.
then after three days,
i reached over,
closed her eyes,
and the stone
never rolled away.

Virtuoso

I don't know
why I play the piano.
It is something
inside of me.
I like
moving people
if I feel them
with me.
I am one
of the six
finalists in this open
competition.
My concerto
is so beautiful.
Much applause.
Thank you.
I don't enjoy
playing the piano.
I just enjoy
the music
like reading
old love letters
in the quiet
of my room
and I hear nothing
but the music.

Shalom Healthy Hair and Beauty Salon

Sometimes fantasy is the best way to get through life.
Has that always been your wish? To be beautiful, have
healthy hair and peace? But you know there are wars
going on and cleansing of a different kind and cities
completely removed from the map. We can all make up a
new life or a world as pedestrian as some imagine the
1950s were like. You have a storm inside of you
that brings the cool air from the west into
collision with warm Gulf air from the south
and we wait for the orange rectangle on the
weather channel map to cover
our part of the country. It will come, as it always does,
in the night or the gray of the morning,
with cloud to ground lightning, hail
the size of your fist, and mythical rain.
The tourists come by to see what beauty and peace
really look like. They catch a glimpse of the debris
left from last night and only watch how you make
beautiful healthy hair in this place called shalom.
They ask a couple of questions and then move on
to the next attraction because the bus will leave soon.
You have impressed another group and collected
some loose change which you are saving for a new sign
for your shop. Your drinking has been getting worse
and you keep asking the neighbors for money
because the baby needs diapers or medicine
to get through the night.

Where you go is your business. I have
my life, my own storms and distractions.
This is a usual day, a tapestry of how you know
what you know. It's a good place to be subversive,
to comb your hair, stand under the lightning,
shake your fist at the myth of our popular attraction.

The Deathbed Edition

You must turn back
the bed for yourself
and remember–
this is English
we are learning.
Elizabethan.
The heaviness in your
chest like a river
damned.
The married self,
as if he were different,
watches the family
of the past. The hour
before dinner
was for the violin.
It is Epiphany now
when flesh and blood
are made known
and there is hope
from childhood
to free the waters.

Silence

You never know what may run in your family.
There have been so many rumors, incomplete
documents, and sepia photographs that disintegrate
at your touch. There could be any number
of causes related to heredity, or even heresy, for health
beyond family or legal records. Brain activity
or any involuntary muscle movement
is especially silenced over the years
like an affair between two prominent people
in the community or the deformed child hidden
in the room above the garage. But you could try
a variety of religious or healing medicines to ease
the pain of such a crazy time. Although you have said
you want to know why, at your age and place in life,
why this particular affliction. You cannot place
the exact beginning of the symptoms and sometimes
they disappear for a couple of days only to return
often at very awkward times. And it has been
a companion of yours for so long that you would think
someone in the family would have some history
or medical fact growing on the family tree–
except the family tree withered like the fig tree
at the voice of God. Maybe this is what happened
with the brothers, sisters, cousins, and all
the relatives discovered only after the death
of your father. It could have been that God's voice
destroyed what might have been an answer

for so many of your questions. If you believe
that sentence you are open to charges of heresy
which runs in the family, or so you are told.
Keep the questions from choking you
and that voice from striking you down
and let your long hair glow like a fire
burning, burning, burning.

All the Help We Can Get

This is Kenny Burrell playing "Satin Doll" solo in my red room.
A south wind has been blowing all day strong enough to lift
an ordinary fly ball to left over the fence. It can change
an average life into something significant and it gives
the crowd an excuse to stand, yell, respond according
to the love they have chosen. But there is more to it
than love or some whimsical decision and we seldom
can do it on our own. So we need help. When you walk
along the edge of the river you may want to hold
someone's hand. And simply trying to get through
a particular day some have found that having the other
person slide one finger along your hand is such a gentle
way to be very helpful. Maybe it would be possible even
to lean across the table at the noontime restaurant
and kiss each other instead of using words of assurance.
O, how to believe in the help we need? To believe
means "to give one's heart to." How does that sound?
There is so much to let go of and hold on to at the same
time. And no matter what you think I do not come close
to satin and I know I am not that much of a doll.

Blood Drive Today Only (Door Prizes)

You take the poison to get along throughout the day.
Because of what is in your veins you cannot donate blood
and, therefore, you are not eligible for a prize. You cannot
even wear that red and white sticker on your shirt or
blouse to show that you care about dissenters in this town
or in countries whose names you can't pronounce let alone
spell. You cannot save a life, even of a friend, because
of what is in your veins. You try to put a good face on it
but it really burns you–like a needle when the nurse
talks about a small prick. There's most of the town
flat on their backs dripping blood into plastic tubes
and sucking on oranges. You don't have the right
to take time off from work or even to feel weak.
No chance of a prize, to win anything. Give anything.
So maybe you should look up at the sky and believe
in long, hot baths with a glass of wine and forget
what you cannot give. Or receive. You are floating away
and will soon be able to see much further than it feels
right now. Tonight you did not speak very well but in no
time at all you will stun the town with your words of glass
that could shatter under someone's feet but not
as carefully as you step. You are beautiful
even without a prize, an orange, or having to bleed.

One of My Earliest Memories

Someone needs to interrupt me. I have talked about myself
so long I'm sure you must have other things to do. We
    have been
under siege for months and now you come to interview us.
My family has disappeared, been buried in what might
    just as well
be a mass grave. I stayed with them as long as I could,
    gave
them all the comfort anyone could expect but all around
    us it felt
like an earthquake, the earth rolling with each shock. Yes,
    the rumors
are true; I did bury them but I thought it was the right
    thing to do.
In fact, it was what I wanted to do, I had trained all my life
to make it to that moment. You can quote me if you wish.
    Everything
is for the record now. Except after I talk about it I always
    get sick
to my stomach. Today, just sitting at my desk at the office,
    it felt
like a heart attack. Now I realize that is exactly what it was.
    Do you
want me to keep going? Let me ask you a question: Can
    you
get someone's attention when they are dead? Look at the
    cross

on the wall. Does it mean anything to you? No one has asked
    me
what it means. I think it means we live a violent life and when
    Jesus
wanted the little children to come to him was it a blessing
    when he
touched them or did something happen we'll never know
    about?

Midnight

I was looking
for a snack
opened the refrigerator
door and found
the jar of preserves
made by that
kind old woman
(name escapes me now)
who died
four years ago.

The Comedic Applicant

There is no way of knowing how funny each of the
applicants can be until we see them face to face.
How often can you listen to the same jokes from standup
comics who have no gift? It's as funny as walking down
Amsterdam towards St. John the Divine and remembering
how none of us smiled when we first read Dante. Can you
understand where you have been traveling and why this
comedic applicant is really very dangerous to society
and you in particular? Read the references, look at the
resume more closely. There is no gift here. No purgatory.
Except you cannot forget those days of living in your car
and getting to the news room just in time to type out
your story about the slums of Saigon for deadline. You
were it. And now you are trying to judge the potential
for humor in each of these applicants. There is no
gift here. But you are the one to make the decision, you
are responsible. This does not feel very gentle, more
like an axe handle to break up a fight. That's what
this poem is. From this prison I can see another prison
and there are always fights breaking out and now
we have to find eloquence wherever we can because the war
is getting closer. You need to decide whether it is
St. John, or Dante, or Saigon. You know the rules
of this art; it's all in the timing, nothing to do with soul
or heart, only survival before the cross, on your knees, in the dirt.

The Average Level of Happiness

NOTHING A LITTLE LIGHTENING WOULDN'T FIX

You are complaint driven.
One thing
after another. The world
situation. Your own
longings
unmet. Not even wanting
to be touched
yet some people
still believe
in love—
like a little lightening
wouldn't fix that!

1.
Traveling

SORRY

for the quiet
not sure how the juggling
(jugular?)
is going to last
next thing that gives
isn't going to be
me again laugh

TRAVELING

I got up to explore the house
and the one night
I stayed in Vienna.
I went down to the bar
of the small hotel near the airport
hoping for dinner but the kitchen
was closed. Another American
and one quiet German
began to buy me beers. I followed
their example. Soon there were wars
and rumors of war. We each told honest stories
about our kids, marriages, divorces. How we had done our
best. The German was using one word sentences. The other
American, from Chicago, had a life-time:
"All I wanted to do was teach
high school history and coach baseball. But I got married
and thought I should own the world, you know,
take care of the family." We exchanged business cards with
email addresses—even the German. We exchanged
all of the regrets of life like poison. I managed
to walk back to my third-floor room,
thinking of the morning flight
back to Riga and the poison
I was trying not to swallow.
Earlier in the day as we landed I saw a combine
cutting the grain next to the runway. Just like home.

Then I heard the trumpets of Krakow, saw the ovens at Aushwitz,
the clowns in Warsaw, the beggars in St. Petersburg,
the fake Modigliani in Ahkmatova's room.
I had to explore the house like a country
making me crazy
one word
at a time.

NOTE FROM SARAJEVO

I know that many
of my best friends
are dead in that river.
It carries them
even now, as I watch,
into the larger
river flowing so gently,
stone by stone,
under or over
a bridge, ancient
and lovely. Then
it all floods
into confusion.
That is what
I remember
of the details
of childhood.

TRUTH

I went to a movie
tonight for the first time
since July. I was in
Sarajevo then and
saw American Pie
with subtitles in Bosnian.

Maybe you think
I am lying about
not seeing a movie for
so long. I would only
lie if I was sure my
own annihilation was at
stake or if a close friend
dying asked me—
"Don't I look beautiful?"

MARINA

I am the only child
in my family
although now I am grown.
My father still comes to my apartment
to make "adjustments."
Sometimes I am not happy
with what he does because
he asks my preference
and still does it his own way.
I studied at Columbia
and would like to go back to New York.
I remember during Soviet times
the shops were empty
and the black market in Riga
was very active and expensive.
But my mother, who had little money,
went to the market
and bought me a dress
from a package—the word we use
for something from the black market.
What color? I remember—
it was blue and yellow.
It had little squares.
I was eight years old.
The place where the boats go?
That is my name.

PROSPECT

I don't know
how much of this
I am making up.
Does it matter to you?
I may not have
the facts straight.
I remember a toilet,
white, on its side
on the grass between
the sidewalk
and Prospect Ave.
Maybe it was a shrine
although I think
it was more of
an accident.
We all have those,
god, we all
have those.
Love? Yes, it seems
we have that, too.
But am I making
that up as well?
I am always the one
Who says: I love you.
Or am I also making
that up? I'm tired.
I am tired of drifting
into places
Where everyone only

Takes back what
They never said,
Or meant or
could possibly feel.
We all try to make up
For so much.

BALKAN GHOST

The daylight distracts me.
I had the most luscious
tangerine last
night, something impossible
after dawn.
Then you asked me
about the rest
of my world.
It was like
the sun crashing
through my front door
and that was my answer.

KRAKOW

The rain is falling
all around the city.
You follow the map
past the trumpet
tower, the internet
cave, across the bridge
into Schindler's
neighborhood. You visit
the small museum
in the pharmacy.
The rain has stopped
like love that is
no longer true.
You make a donation
to the museum
and move on.

VINETA'S STORY

These are our protected stones.
Each has a story,
really a life—
of its own.

One had a lover
who turned out to
live very
unlike a stone.

FROM THE FRONT PORCH

So
are you looking up
into the night sky,
watching the stars
naming the constellations—
wondering about Israel
and Palestine, all the children
running through
cemeteries to escape
gunfire—
Afghanistan and which
country is next?
I am.

TAMMY WYNETTE IN RIGA

I catch that voice in a café near our apartment
where I go to read the paper and sip dark coffee
by myself late in the afternoon. Tammy brings me

to my own memories good enough
for any country classic. They grab hold of me like drinkin'
and cheatin'—the whole story.

Where do you imagine
yourself along the timeline? Here in this country
dawn comes so early—often
just as I am falling asleep. Then any memories,
dreams or nightmares must be set in place

before the light sends them
back to the woods or near the Baltic ghosts
of hideous crimes buried to the tide. You are
just beginning to feel
the panic—home is closer to the country lyric
than you thought. So much depends

on the chemistry
that attracts life, love and the active dying
we see all around us during these long days, short nights.
We each have such memories.
It is not hope hanging on these walls.

VALENTINE'S DAY

Someone said today that travel
To one of those romantic countries
Like France—no, the word was

romance—would be just what
she needed. But then the talk
moved to other parts

Of the world like the Dalmatian
Coast or better yet the Virgin
Islands. We laughed about

the double meanings of the place
names and whether she would find
romance or just more heartache

or dogs or virgins. And then she
decided there was nothing to lose
as she grew more serious about leaving.

INTO THE WORLD

You name
your child
"where the hawks fly"
or, in other words,
the heavens.
How heavy the head
that wears the crown.

SAYING GOODBYE

You gave your skin
without question
or tears.

Like a spring
rain you fell
into the ground

where the grass
was very pale
from loss
and the death of the sky.

OBEY RIVER

You fall asleep
and go straight
to ashes. And the day
you awake with your skin
wrinkled like a small
unloved animal
is the day you decide
to call it quits. You
make a clear decision
and even the weather agrees.
There is a man, a voice,
on the morning radio saying to you:
It's all been downgraded,
now it's just another
north Atlantic storm.

CULTURE (Kultura)

Everyone knows Verdi
needs to be heard
in Italian
but with Wagner
any language will do it.
After using it
for a week now
I noticed today
that the urinal
has instructions
in three languages.
Wagner must have been here.

THE GLASS MOUNTAINS

are in Oklahoma
where there is
never just
someone.

As in Andalusia,
the Muslim heartland,
everything becomes
breakable.

SREBRENICA

she seemed
uncomfortable—as if
she didn't know
what to do
with her body
which is why

NIGHT FLIGHT

I brushed my teeth in St. Louis but that fresh
mint flavor did not make it halfway
through the flight to Baltimore. Behind me I
overheard someone say—

        I got married a month ago
        and it still feels like one big slumber party.

There were other conversations along this journey
in the dark. I was trying to read, write,
work on the purpose of the meeting I would attend.
But memories kept floating around like the clouds
I was told were outside the plane. In Riga I remembered
the way the women held each other
just walking down the street – arm in arm – and the flags

        to acknowledge the most recent
        liberation. Then a march down the main
        streets to celebrate a hockey victory over
        the United States. I swear I didn't know
        as I leaned out my window cheering and waving
        to the crowd so happy to have brought down a
            giant.

Who knew the difference here? Don't hold me
to what I say. Any god or angel in her
right mind would make some lame excuse for taking us
this far.

You might be thinking of poor,
limping Jacob, but hell he got a slumber party, a fight,
and a new name – like marriage for some.
We are getting close to Baltimore, they say, the final descent,
and you just keep finding yourself wanting.

STUFFED

Pastrami is a verb, she said,
a way of treating anything.
Somehow the meaning is
traced back to Vilna or what
we now call Vilnius.
and there's a rabbi in the story.
It goes on and on about the first deli
in New York, and mustard and the many
secrets of the process. You never really know how
it all ends because, look what happened
to the Jews in Vilnius, and Riga—all over.
Now we are watching as Palestinian
children die in what they thought was home.
It's the present, violent tense of the verb.
The grammar of hell and this hell
is not the absence of birds.
It's a way of treating anything.

PASSION SUNDAY

Any town named Hooker,
eighty residents,
must have at least one
motel, maybe two. The land
here is so flat
you can see it
disappear before your eyes.
Those who remain
on this horizon
shout in the heat
of passion, "Save us!"

AMERICA WEST

He kept listening
for the unknown.
He wanted to
be on a plane
surrounded by
a language he did
not understand, that
would attract his
attention rather than
interrupt his rest.
There is so much quiet
in what is not
obvious. Another tongue
would support his head
in its hand, a new breath
might reach his heart
with fresh blood and,
in other words, move him—
move him through
the air.

TO LET YOU KNOW I'M

moving to the land
of David Lynch
to battle suburban
spread and those
with fears of leaving
the city to visit
old friends
come visit me
in other words
as of tomorrow
evening
I will
be living

2.
FRANTIC

WISHING WELL

Don't you wish sometimes
you could just take away one night?
It would make such a difference
in all that has happened since
in your life. You could walk
without bending your head
toward the street. You might
even be able to tell
your story to someone
you admire without the fear
of disappointment
greying their face.

THE TONGUE RIVER

The water moves
along as slowly
as mud and invites
you to come along—
to bathe
in its healing
dance—to lose
all thought
of the world
around and around
you—follow
the river down
to the sea
and you will
hear the singing
of blue music
from the delta mouth.

THE WAY YOU ARE

You burn bridges for a living.
Wait, that is wrong,
or half-right—your
life is blood
and flesh, like the rest
of us, good and bad, who's
to judge? You stand on the edge
wanting this, glad for that,
with less and less to laugh
about. Then you see someone,
meet someone, even imagine, and the edge
moves. You laugh
like the rest of us.

MAGGIE'S STORY

She just would never answer.
No matter what you tried
She would lazily cross
Her arms and say something
Completely strange,
Avoiding the point. She
Might say:
It feels like rain,
Salt-rain that stings
My eyes. Then she
Would be gone
As if someone pulled her
Out of the car
Without a sound. What
Is left is the story
She wrote:
One sunny day
There was a girl.
There was.

READING THE SUNDAY PAPER

I am tripping again
with my mouth. The stress
brings it on
and you make a joke
about easing up,
taking my time.
But you have your journey
and it isn't mine.
And you have your words
and they aren't mine.
What is it like,
I ask, to look
yourself in the eye?
Where are your demons?
The ad in the paper
reads: Learn French
In Your Car.
You ask: didn't we all?

DADA

You often say
"don't hold
your breath"

as if I can
do anything else
under all this water.

RIVERS

I love your rivers. They move
over the stones
and smooth the rough
edges of centuries
with Homeric courage.

They drop
hundreds of feet
as beautiful
as they are deep. Then rage
through valleys

and narrow
ravines with a vengeance
that keeps us
twisting and swirling
in frantic romance.

LAUNDRY

Everyone wants to be made
happy with the clever
manipulation of nerve
endings like washing our clothes
and barely fitting it all
in the machine. We pour
that white powder
into the large opening,
push the right buttons,
hear the rush of hot
water over those dirty clothes
without a body. Then
comes the pleasure
of still being alive
when the wash is over
and the dryer
gives up its sweet odor
in a warm tumble.

VALENTINE

Something always
seems to be missing
from the body
of your voice.
With Valentine's Day
coming you don't
know what to do
with your own strength
in the face
of such good feelings.
They move so quickly
you can't catch them
like small birds
loving the entire sky.

TEXAS WOMAN ON TRIAL

The voices said to use a knife
on the children. I thought, no,
too much blood. For months now
I have grown older and older
feeling aches and pains in new
places and losing memory of who
or what I am. My skin has become
very thin as I have thought
about the loss of heart. Some people
say I am very sick, but I still know
how to love even as dark as it gets
just before I fall asleep. Then as I
feel the day behind the pale window
my fingers become ice and my eyes
want to stay closed. I hear
the toaster calling out to me—then
the orange juice, cereal, the brown bag
of coffee in the freezer. I know
the truth. It's supposed to set
us free even in my country
where the morning sky shines beyond anyplace
I have ever been. Until now.

DANTE

You have spent the day
following the dead. Carla Del Ponte
is your hero. You have traced
the twisted paths like children
working on their book of mazes. And for them
and you it has been a long journey
facing obstacles like very hot stones,
storms exploding
from skies half-blue,
reluctant travelers who
suddenly fall in love
slowing the crowd with their obvious passion
and driving you
to your wit's end. But you
continue writing because
these are the damned
we are talking about
and they may rebel
at the slightest provocation.
It is tempting to just disappear
among the bones of the earth
making a mass grave for yourself.
But you are no war crimes general,
you are a writer, 14th century, Italian,
and this may be your best work.
So, now, go find Beatrice,
undress her, love her, love her to death
before it's too late.

WITNESS PROTECTION PLAN

You have spent
the past hour
holding life
at bay.

Changing names,
lefthand,
right,
moving from
hotel to cottage
and back,
keeping your identity
so much a secret
that even the mirror
is surprised.

You have now
taken to putting
perfume in
strategic places.

ENOUGH

In the night
all the shadows
break the limbs
of sleeping trees

and death just
steps where it will—
over you, over me,
out into the sea

THE MUSICIAN

When I was
a young girl
and first heard
the cello

it sounded
so sad.
I believed
she needed me.

WRITER'S ALMANAC

Today is Langston Hughes' birthday.
Born in Joplin
and then the music beneath
the skin, the music that dances
at good news and when the bad
comes weeps with those
in sorrow. Follow the music,
follow the music, follow
the music. Then you will see
through the smoke in the room
someone lovely to move
with you across the old floor
stained with fear and laughter.

AN ACCUMULATION OF BRUISES

In every room of the
house you fall against
another sharp object that
adds one more bruise. The
skin takes on

an array of colors
and a life of healing. By then
more wounds appear, layer
upon layer of tissue, day and night.

THE NEST

They count the twigs
in the nest
as they make their home
in the highest
tree around. Then down
and bits of paper
to add that soft touch
they thought love
could not do without.

They look at each other—
the wind picks up
the loose pieces lifting
everything into the sky.
Soon the snow falls
and the ground and the trees
all become still,
quiet, and quiet.

HALFWAY HOUSE

You always hear
the street—get the weather
from the clerk at the
gas station—it's going
to get worse.

I would rather
believe it will only
be slight flurries
from now on.
Can you make

relationships or
just take hostages?
It's an old question
thrown in my face
whenever I look
at you.

Back to the house—
or half of it. We have
divided the rooms
with interior walls
so everyone has

some space
of their own. But violation
comes so quickly.
What sticks in your throat
this morning?

THE PATRIOT

O, what a night!
The mighty prophet of day,
the heat and all of her
strength has gone
for even a sliver—
grave of light.

Soon you will see
how the majesty
of just being
in this beautiful country
makes the child in you
fight for a way to be free.

A GESTURE

The final roll
of the sea
swam onto
your lap,
kissed you like
a long-lost
Gulag relative,
on each side
of the face
and you smiled.

The reason
for life
and death belongs
to that gesture,
a turn or move
of the body,
that shows you
the importance
of water and love.

You stood
ready for more
even though you said—
don't hold me
to what I say—
then stretched out

on the sand and waited
for the twist
or turn
that you knew
would rise
like the skin.

A WORD FROM THE WISE

You can only
Live with so much
Beauty. Crafted
Of solid and pine veneer
This casual queen
Has a distressed
Wash finish.

I am such a queen!
Without the need for a king
I can make a new face
Pressing my life
Against the window.

I am such a queen!
Craving some soft skin,
Less anxiety about
My health
And the useless wish
To have my anger
Turned toward someone
Other than you.

3.
SILHOUETTE

COME THE NIGHT

In one dream
I am beginning to learn
To smoke in another
I find a lamb gutted
From ribs to tail.

It could be some
Small rebellion
Or a feeling of
Losing my courage
Or even giving up on

Whatever kept me
Alive. On the other
Hand we could turn
Tragedy into the comedy
We believe in so well.

OPTIONS FOR EPISCOPALIANS

My vocal cords are in my stomach but
that is not an option for you.
I have a culture—maybe African—
on the dry land in the midst of waters,
a shadow sparkling all around me
like sweet dreams on a given night.

We have been under siege for years
and now you come to interview us.
My family has disappeared, it is
complicated but not as much as you
may think. They have been buried
in what has been called a mass

grave. You can picture a skull,
you can picture a mother holding
the skull, you can picture a child,
then put it all together. You agree?
No words for it, only a stomach
on dry ground. Not even a dream?

EPIPHANY

Trying to drift off
to sleep the bed
became a raft
you were clinging to
as a wave
lifted your side
of the lashed-together,
rough-planked
final hope.
You could see
into the dark
open mouth of
the monster
so hungry.
You never
wanted to be swallowed.

WARNINGS

They call it
a storm cell

and left alone
it does so much
damage. More so
than if joined
by another storm
as it scatters parts
and pieces of lives
across the land,
your face, and all
that you put
in the way
to protect
what you believed
you were worth.

THE OCCUPATION MUSEUM

—Riga, Latvia

No one

in the photographs
is smiling
except the young
people who
are, perhaps,
just in love.

FALLING

I had a dream
of finding an old Miles Davis
album called
Sketches of Spain.
It was such a surprise that I
doubted—in the dream—
that inside the cardboard
case Sketches
would really
be there. I was sure
someone would slip
an obscure concerto
or Manilow's
greatest hits inside and make off
with the real music.
I bought the album
without checking
despite my doubts
because I have always
fallen for the beauty
of a silhouette.

THE CHRISTMAS CARD

See the red wings
on the angel? The
originals are glass
and able to break
any heart that moves
between one deep breath
and another. They
remind me of the blood
that warms cold skin
when there is love
in the shadows
and the straw.

THE ROOT OF YOUR RECOLLECTION

Take the last smart move
you made
and go the way
anger throws you
out of the house.

Take another shot
at the face
staring the life
out of you.

If you still miss me
always remember
the blade of time
sharp as one word.

THE FIRST SNOW

It's all age-related. In the next bed the old lady
is yelling for LeRoy and swearing at him for just
disappearing like that. They will move her soon,
there has not been a change in the weather today so the
nurses in ER and on other floors are bracing for a
full house—a busy day and night. With the dry
air, the prairie dust, the snow, people make plans
for a room at the hospital just in case they have
symptoms of distress or a family member needs
immediate attention. It's all age-related: The discount
on meals. A free personal-items bag with hospital logo.
The magazine with tips for good health. But they
can't move the yelling woman right now,
no bed available. Everyone needs something. Help me,
she is shouting. LeRoy, that sonofabitch, is gone, all of him.

INTENSIVE CARE

The verb for living or dead
is conditional. It reads our lips
in silent witness to unspeakable crime
or lasting love that cannot taste
even this flavored sentence
or these fleshed-out words.

Time and time again
we find the night so dark
we close our eyes and bathe
our fetal body barely
taking a breath in an effort
to get out alive.

Whatever animal you dreamed
of being or fought in the cave
of your nightmare-sleep
now whispers to you
escape, escape across the river.
So, you went north where the snow

was cold and funny in its own
way. It just did not seem
to enjoy your intrusion.
Someone reaches over the bed
and closes your eyes. Your love
weeps, weeps across the river.

A LIFETIME

Harold just lost his wife
of 46 years, 6 days,
and 5 minutes.
O, how love runs
us ragged.

THE AVERAGE LEVEL OF HAPPINESS

You were seeing
If your heart was
Beating crooked.
It would take some
Expert to test
Your blood and muscle
Tone for going on.
Sometimes you can picture
Yourself at the beginning
Of a new light
With music at the table, flowers,
And no one to taste
Your past lives.
As you approach this new age—
It will give breath
To the one who has done
So many funerals for
Those younger now
Than you. Then your
One thought as the party candles
Go up in smoke—
I don't wish to be broken open again
Ever in this way.

Aint Leavin' This House

Rough Dried

LESSON #1

I trust no one
with my name
in their mouth.

A NIGHT ON BROADWAY

Ain't leavin' this house rough dried.
You put on the ironed skirt I fixed

for you last night and the good blouse
your Grandma gave you for church.

You ain't goin' outside with your hair
lookin' like steel wool from the hardware

store, you brush it down and out and do
your teeth while you're at it. And your face

ain't too good either with those
marks and cuts, you fix up those scars

or no man will want you. Then those
earrings need to go, put on the long

bright ones I got you in Vegas
cheap but they attract the money men

like dirt flies. Those lips need softenin'
so use this gloss from Walgreen's

just for your color and shape. Now
stand up straight. With those eyes

and hips and long fourteen year old
legs you bring me back some real gold.

SOMEWHERE

a left wrist bone is on the ground
next to a leg from a woman
waiting for bread just moments ago. A baby
blown from her mother's arms
is found crushed under a jeep
half a block down the street.
There are toes and ankles for the stray
dogs to steal. My job
is to get the other poor
bastard to die
for his country. We
are all doing well.

FUTURE HOME OF GLAD TIDINGS CHURCH

Bending your knees to the floor
you pray. After that you walk to a book store
for coffee and then wander into the
children's section. All the Easter
specials are on display but you find the classics that you
remember hearing and reading a lifetime ago. God played
with you then and made you laugh
and taught you games, words, how to sing,
both of you being just children.

SOME SAVIOR

This alley leads to a wall
with the message: To be saved,
you must shoot six times
into a small brown house,
the one on the corner of 16th
and Erie. Of course, only the select few
can read the ancient script. At 12:14 a.m.
it is Easter morning, the cross
has been carried, dropped,
carried again. The nails remain.
The women mourn and the men have disappeared
hours ago. It is time to go for a drive
looking for some savior's shadow
flickering like a candle
behind the curtained window
about to be shattered.

BLOOD TEST

The doctor called this morning
with the news – perfect blood,
vampire heaven, get out the cross
and the dagger. Tonight will be
wild on the town, we'll have to watch
everyone. Times Square is full of the stranger
and lovely, black-coated lovelies, with scarves
swirling like war-time snow. With perfect blood
you can be entertained, photographed, walk
the red carpet into posh blinding lights.

STEALING "THE SCREAM"

-- BOSNIA, 2004

I watch the men play chess
in Sarajevo. The pieces are large,
the size of the legless man
begging at the wall of the mosque.
He plays the accordion to attract
extra donations. It may be music
to the ears of thousands buried
in local football fields. It may not be music
at all to those who hate
the musician. And to those
involved in stealing "The Scream,"
that painting my granddaughter
copied in chalk for my refrigerator door,
the painting meant to haunt
the lives so many of us missed
by such remembrances. So
surrender now to the authorities
or we will take all
of your women and children,
put them in some sacred place,
tie their wrists behind
their backs and let
the building burn. On second thought
keep the painting and the music
will split your heart
like an ax to dry wood.

DEAR EDWARD

Thank you for the message
about your mother and
your life at the Boston
hospital. Some of it
sounds so familiar. The green
bile in the pan, the strength
in her dying smile, instructions
to give her the most
comfort possible. Today
I talked with a ten year old
girl from the next block whose
auntie was shot and killed
a few days ago. Brianna gave me
a hug and a smile, I responded
with same. I now pass Brianna's smile
and hug on to you. She would
approve. We all know something
about the green –
and there will be
other colors. The winter solstice
is coming, Hanukkah
began Saturday. Both
announce a change
in the light.

NO CHILD LEFT BEHIND

He has a shark smile as if he would lend
you anything. Put it all out on the table
so he can see it like a wound to tend

from crossing the seller at Piatt and 14th Street.
His name was never given, it was forced on him
by someone in the dark you would not want to meet.

Flesh to flesh, all those men gathered in their stoned way
with her young children all in one small room waiting
their turn at the television. But the men all stay

and use those children for the toys that crack
as they are opened. It is a quiet evening, a quiet
house, no one would know you took that pretty snack.

O WHAT LOVE

O what love does to an old heart.
From my study window

looking down on Hillside St.
I see the homecoming Escort vans,

the blue light specials flashing
their way through late morning traffic

leading a funeral procession. My first thought,
of course, should I have been officiating,

but only a few people I know have died in
the past few days, o what love. It is

the middle of Lent. What will Good Friday
bring you and me? Or later that weekend

we could hope for some ordinary
resurrection. You have a blood clot

in your leg that splits in two. Both pieces
go to the heart but because of the

brokenness you live.
The heart cannot take large

constrictions but perhaps small ones.
The broken blood has saved you.

WOMAN REGRETS KILLING HUSBAND

I was drunk and you know
what happens when
you get drunk. Tequila.
It was stupid. I did
a stupid thing. I loved
Roger. He was my future.
He has a good family.
Now I've lost everything. No
money. No family. I deserve
the most severe penalty
and the key thrown away.
We were just at home one evening
on the west side. He was tired,
drinking beer. I just walked
across the room to the closet,
brought out the shotgun
and pulled the trigger.
You know what happens.
Tequila by the grace of God.

STARI MOST

Mostar, Bosnia-Hercegovina

Beauty
is built from mistakes.
So from
the Neretva
all progress begins with
photographs, memory,
arguments
of residents,
on to the gathering
of tools and
stone. Any beautiful
bridge is
a human body
and now you
are lifting your broken
bones – leg, skull –
out of the water,
standing on your own,
solid finally from centuries
of longing to move
from one side
to the other.
It is a long walk
and we could lose
our balance.
This mistake, we fear,
may not last forever.

PREACHER

Drifting from here to there,
from the hotel to the street
preaching
corner to corner.
Women like that. They might give you
a meal
but not a room
for the night. Religion
is one thing, preaching
something else
again. So many of us
spend lives
with an eye
over our shoulder but you
decided: "God watches my back.
My eyes are dead in front."

BETHLEHEM

I am doing my job.
Is it true
that advent is about God
not forgetting?
For nineteen years
people have been
coming to me with lives
dying as much as
could be expected.
But now
everyone has left
the building.
I will go soon,
get a glass of wine,
disappear into
my own quiet love,
a couch the color
of wheat, almost human,
manger-like,
without the star.

HOLDING ON

I like the idea of what
the rest of you deny
out of hatred and do
something good with it.
I'd like to live in the garden
although you may not. I'm afraid
I need directions
otherwise I may be lost –

"otherwise" – good title for
a book of poems

otherwise
I'm afraid.

THE SMILE

My grandson says
Hobby Lobby is evil. I agree.
You know it just by walking through
the doors, not hell exactly, but
a frightening place filled with beads,
plants that were never alive, paint by number,
green ware, racks of frames with photos
of smiling young girls whose fate
no one knows. The store clerks
remind me of characters in the old
zombie movies – pale, lifeless, eyes never
blinking. What is their life story? What debts
do they have? Will someone greet them
at home and say, "I love you?" Or is that
just a hobby we all practice from time
to time to make it to the next
person who smiles, seeming to like you,
and asks: "May I help?"

"But who can endure...?"

-- Malachi 3:2

This is your face
at Christmas. The house
is so sensitive
and, in the photograph,
even looks like you.

Under the tinseled
tree you find your first
rifle. But you are not
sure if it is real
or another toy.

Soon you are
amazed by what
has been let
loose inside.

THE PROPHET

Jeremiah
reminds me
of my husband. He keeps
talking to me
after my eyes
are shut.

"My day went
like this…, and then
this happened…."

Then the damn angel
proclaimed:
"Do not fear."
I say:
What kind
of advice
is that?

A ROSE FOR ELLEKE

Granddaughter, b. 9-22-03

This rose

bred for

red

has fragrance,

many,

for grace, gift

or gripe

as life begins

at seven pounds,

seven ounces

breaking the quiet

like diving

out of water.

THE DEEPEST WATER I KNOW

I am 58 years old
and eating tuna out of a can
for supper. I have
a real job
with health,
other benefits
and respect
at least from some.
So now
the wine.

MASS GRAVE

You have a special touch
with the dying. It's the living
that give you trouble. Maybe it is knowing
that death will take them
out of your danger zone into
a file folder with vital information
hand-written – year by year.
The living take a toll that keeps you
reaching into your pockets for change
and your heart pays forever. It was cold
from the north today like winter which it is
to the soul, to the bone. The body is an image
just below the earth like a photo
shuttered from the sky.

HOW TO

Being a parent, yes,
is hard. Being
a child,
nearly
impossible.

THE DIVORCE

I'm afraid of stuff.
Of sleeping and not.
The radio news and music in the dark and silence.
Being left behind when the adults are gone.
Your tears that make mine stop.
Are you sad is not a question but a way of life.
I feel myself floating in the sky looking down for food.
There is Africa from the moon.

FIRST STEP

My ten year old grandson
woke me up from my Sunday
afternoon nap. He
gently put his arms around
me – let me know
that dinner was ready
downstairs. Then he crawled
up on the bed himself
with his back to me
and looked out the window
at the lonely winter trees
trying to make family.
I stirred and sat on the edge
of the bed. He came over to me,
took my arm saying
let me help you, grandpa.
Outside the trees were
fighting a cold wind,
struggling to make sense
of so many changes.
When we reached the
bedroom door
my grandson let go
of my arm, smiled, and said
now, you're on your own.

OBOE SOLO

*"As Van Gogh understood, gold comes
in many forms: the best is art."*

-- Madeline DeFrees

She played her chosen
instrument

carefully as if
Mozart might be

guarding his concerto
off-stage.

I came to hear this music
live because of a free ticket

and to keep my own art
from crawling out from under

my skin and away. I was not playing.
The world is not so much with us and you can hope

to God your addiction is not to heaven. The saved
still do the stuff

in the right crowd. I watched her
and it was like waiting for the snake

to rise from the basket
and strike.

THE WORKOUT

Shadow boxing
while sitting there at your
desk writing one
word next
to another. Blood
pounding in your ears,
arms pushing weights
to their limit. Sweat
stinging your eyes
as you pace around the ring
gathering strength,
another broken nose.
All the memory gone to anger.
Sister, you need
a punching poem.

CONSTELLATION

I looked up at the high
desert sky
and saw eight
of the seven sisters.
Then your love,
out loud, released
in a moment
which is why I stayed quiet –
discretion being the better
part of distress.

POSTCARD FROM MEXICO

You have traveled the ruins,
danced,
studied the romance
of the words,
and still this love
is as quiet
as paper.

HER MADNESS

I would go raving
mad if the only
person I talked
to all day
was me, pointing
with her hand
to the general area
of her heart. It's
dangerous memory
keeps
her fingers
crossed
a distant second
a good morning
better evening
finally wine.

SLJIVOVICA

You called and said you
would be late
for everything. Then turned
to the small glass
of plum brandy after
talking with a husband who
wants a divorce
and his wife
who doesn't.

She cried, he did not.
She spoke, he was silent.
She won't be touched, he gave up trying.

It seems they are both
late for everything, too, no longer
dizzy in love
just madly dividing up the furniture
and their daughter.

CONCERTINA WIRE

-- *"God bless the child who's got his own...."*
(Holiday and Herzog)

There are two
institutions for the poor:
The military
and prison. In each case
they are surrounded
by circles of gleaming
silver concertina wire.
It is the music of
their place in life
where so often
this and that don't
go the way they ought.
Like today finding
the words, "Kill him?"
in a child's handwriting on stray
paper from the after
school program. One ten year old
girl told me she is
too old to dream any more. The music
continues on little
scraps of paper, notes for a song
from the children of concertina.

THERE'S MORE TO KANSAS

For the second
time this summer
an alligator was found
here in Wichita. Three
to four feet long so they say
it must have been dumped
along the road
by its former owner.
Keep in mind then
that Kansas is much more
than the Wizard
of Oz and Dorothy,
as we mourn
the tragic
passing of Toto.

MEMORIAL DAY

Kansas – 2005

I went to Spangles for
my Memorial Day
hamburger, fries and
shake. My # was
478 although I
was the only customer.
Alice took my order,
gave me a cup for a coke
but I reminded her
of the chocolate shake.
She apologized. She looked like
she was almost happy
to be there. It was a job, she said,
but it was a job. I did not
know her but could tell
by her face she was
a veteran of many wars.
I order you to give a flag, neatly folded,
to a close relation, twenty-one gun salute, taps
played by a soldier in uniform with a real bugle.
And after she is buried put a small
gravestone on the ground above her to remember
the many assaults she faced
alone with no weapons
or army of support. On the stone put
her last words to me:
"Here you go, hun."

FINALLY

When I finally memorized
the spelling of Mediterranean
I believed I knew everything
about the entire sea.

THE TIJUANA CITY DUMP

Nothing special.
Children look as ancient
as recently discovered
stone caves. White
dust whispers lost
virgin soil over the
cardboard beds laid
out for the night. Heavy fog
covers those of us
staring back at you.
Finding a coin or a
stray pear means
everything.

"BEING ZEUS"

In Memoriam: Kenneth Koch

He is a curious dog. He goes to the trash
in my study and pulls out old poems or fragments
to inspect or chew. Sometimes he seems to know
exactly what he is looking for but usually
he is just – curious. Being the god
of gods is not easy. There is actually
not a lot of independence and so much is
expected of you. Sit for this treat, go
only in the backyard, yes, you have to
be on the leash, don't steal the sandwich
from the kitchen counter, off the couch
I'm here, you're in the way of the television,
the news with roadside bombs and strangled lovers.
Being Zeus during these times is tough, no one
pays any attention even to your thunder
or bolts of lightning. You should try being Venus.

ROSES

Knowing first hand
what it means
to be human
I can fix
sad roses.
How dare you
try to forget.

"CRESCENDO IN BLUE"

I was really
heart beaten when I saw
with my own eyes
the difference between love
and lust. It was a melody
with notes on the page
and then improvisation
which exploded
in my face
as I went out one door,
she another.
That is the crescendo.
Those are the blues.
I've played
the instruments,
given away the children,
talked to the suicidal
teenager, tried to get
families to hear
each other through
the shouting. Now,
to end some war
or take groceries to
one person dying
from emphysema. Or call the one
I love and get no answer, only:
"What is happening to my phone?"

So much is missed
that wraps us in
its laughter and you thought
you would see each
other today. Try
another dream after
you crawl through this one.

NEAR MISS

Listen as Orpheus
phones the dead
and makes plans
that most have read

or they've seen the film
slip across the screen.
Then a light dress
that most have seen

and enjoyed those legs
shimmering in Hades' light
and the strange fruit
swallowed by the night.

WATCHING THE NEWS

Tonight the dog was wanting to go
for the gutter
every time I let him out. He would
whine and stare at me as I sat in
the red chair trying to watch the news.
He would do that deep throated half-growl
that says – I need the back yard. But then
he would run straight for his special delicacy
which I could not see in the dark. It was cold outside
and beginning to snow. I managed to get him away from
the mystery meal and inside the house
in time to catch a glimpse of the blood on what looked like
the remains of a car on a street in Iraq. Then the news
    was over.

Woman wins gas for life

And this is the second time.
Of course we are all aware of the double meaning.
As she is.
There is her picture on the front page of the paper.
We have other news but those photos are forbidden.
They would invade the privacy of grieving families.
Might demoralize the troops fighting for liberty.
And undermine public support for democracy.
The woman gets $1200. a year for fifty years of gas.
This seems to be a year for winning at any cost.
This seems to be a year for losing at any cost.
There is another photo on the front page, 20 years old,
    national guard.
She graduated high school last year, ran track, gave it
    everything.

MS. TAYLOR

I spent my life
teaching myself to see.
Then with the brush in my mouth
I painted. Sometimes I don't ever need words.
This is no pastoral scene. It is me.
Self-portrait of a naked disabled artist.
That's what I call it. Sometimes I lay the large canvas on
the floor
to get the right angle. The neighbors, next to my studio,
are on the roof
again to get a look inside.

NIGHT JASMINE

That was your
big mistake. You realized
then its better
to be a little lost
than entirely
found. Resurrection
just means things
are not as they seem.
I keep having
to learn that. Can you
smell the fragrance
from the open window? You think
of a place where the jasmine
would be at home
with you. Watch the live,
tilting-to-one-side
man. He is actually
an angel spinning
on the head
of God. Then you remember
the hawks
were really vultures.

LESSON #9

You say, humans aren't meant to be alone --
although we so often
do such harm when together.

LESSON #10

O, John Clare, so many of us
have died to sing
the songs you taught with courage and madness to love.

BACK THERE

Same active molecule, just slightly different
                    side effects.
          Then her smiling eyes
               ask if I hear
what is back there. Back there
                    in the pond.
It's them, the leopard frogs! They have
     stripes somewhere on the face,
they keep the night alive just
a little longer, they remind us of the world
                    beyond what is found
on any average day. There is the
     immortal. It's just
          not for us.

FIRST STORM

You love to stand out
in the cold wind from
the north at night. It
comes from
Colorado and Wyoming
rattling the windows and giving
you hope in the unknown. You know
you can find a new life, a full
light, in the dark of the clouds
off to the north and
the west. It is a mystery
as she asks about
the snow, has it come
yet…no, life is still
on the move, the snow
is craving a
light falling onto
the ground prepared
for anything but this.
Go back, go back, and you
know it is not possible.
It is still dark in
that direction and
life is on the move
past all that we know.

WHISPERING

yellow finches hang
upside down
to get the seeds

of the sunflower
soon they will be
making circles
in the sky

whispering to each other
better to be present
and visible
than absent
and seen.

THE WOMAN FROM TYRE

She wasn't slouching toward you but knowing your face
from her many dreams and dreads she came full force
shouting for good reason
at what you could and better do.

Then you tried to get out of it claiming
the gift was only
for a select few from the right
country, this was a border issue
but she did not buy it. So she kept shouting
and your friends covered their ears
and told you
to get rid of her,
damn woman,
she lives too close
to the sea,
the salt has made her mad.

But the crowds were also watching as always like they had
    digitals and video
so what could you do? It wasn't your gift
to begin with. It really belonged to her
and, thank God, you recognized the truth before
it was too late. So you said, lady,
because of your love, which we will talk about later,
your daughter will not die. She will live to shout
at some other startled and stumbling savior.
That's what he said, just ask his friends,
if there are any left.

FIDDLING

One poet writes of the "horse latitudes"
in the calm of the storm. One lover
strikes a fiddle, finds a lonely
instrument of courage with many
ways to be an artist or a scam. You
make the money you make
from your art. Your lover and others
have a name for you but you have their #.

BOSNIAN FOLK SONG

Walking the streets
of Mostar
late and into
the darkness
on the Croat side
of the river
we sing --
absence being a body
like heaven.

DIMMING

Ashes to ashes
    dust to dust
this \\

is what we do with
    trust ---

dim that thought
        like light
            from your eyes

into the oncoming truck
    or train or ---

as you say
    my love of death

remember
    everyone is an adult
  once
a child
    twice.

GLASS

enough for now
love to make it through
the thoughts not regrets
you had after the sharp words
left your tongue
moved across
my body
and scarred both of us
as if the glass from childhood
cut our skin which
we gave to each other.

SECRETS

You are tired
of all
memory.

You are full
to overflowing
with holding

back tiny
child-like
secrets.

REVENGE FOR RICHARD HUGO, IN MEMORY

You can pretty much count on storms flying in
or out of
Denver like today. Waiting
on the runway as 4 p.m.
darkness blocks our
way to the southwest
and on to Los Angeles.
The pilot talks to the tower.
There must be a way
out and around
the weather. Is there some
message hidden
in this text?
You have the window seat
and write like crazy,
Plath's last day's
worth of frantic poems
because you are trying
to forget how
badly you have
to pee. The two
teenage girls in center
and aisle are asleep.
Others get to go do what they want to do!
You did not choose this seat,
did not pay for this journey.
You were sent, it's part of the job

and you can only afford so much revenge
unlike Brahms toasting the Indians
after Little Big Horn.

A COLD SPRING

The lilacs bloom like the mouth of a long, wild cry.
The fragrance gives the air a cup.
It overflows like the swallowed soft-shell star.
The blossoms, though so much of the world, still appear
    abandoned.
They are silent under a cold midnight sky.
In the morning they come to church, blessing in their
Lenten way, our wild love.

LAST THERAPY BEFORE BOSNIA

The clouds break
as I walk
out the door.
Transference
was working
overtime. Then
she put her hand
on my shoulder, told me
how courageous I was, to be
safe, send emails and write down
the next appointment.

I DREAM OF WHINING

Too old for this shit –
men, women, all like the rest of us
mixing messages for those
we love to confuse
each other. Is there any
other way to fall in
love? It just always… you know
it does, and the timing is so wrong flowers
don't help. And try
giving them away on the street
to people whom you don't
know. They looked at me like
I was some Vodka-crazed gutter
person. I know you have heard this story
before and you even sound bored
between bites
of tortilla chips but that is also why
with such passion I wanted
Sarajevo. It was so much
safer than any lover
with metaphor and logic
that once again forced my heart
to its impotent knees.

LATE WINTER

You've had enough. What
was taken for love
has turned everything inside
out. The inch of snow
meant to wake us up
this morning
never came. The sun
through the window
proclaims a moratorium
on love and darkness.

THE WAR GAME

And the stones
whirl like we are told
the planets must
do above the enemy waiting with carved
wooden guns. The ambush
is set and we are in position to be trapped
and, yes, imagine the stories that will be told
by the victors. That is the way of history,
of conquering heroes. The days fly like the snap
of slingshots and the nights draw lines around
our breathing. It is filth we lie in as we
await our narrated death. Boys being boys. Some follow,
a few lead. In the end it makes no difference
for as we wait the larger artillery is moved into place.
Our mother's cherished babies will all be lost,
unrecognized in the ditches, covered with mud among
leaves.

VIGIL

If it wasn't for the last minute
so much would never get done.
There is something about the closing
moment of possibility, a final
shot from beyond
the 3-point line, the words
"I have to leave now," and
remembering my mother's
four days of last
breath. In that case
not much was done except
a building exhaustion that eight
years later seems to be easing
but who can trust
what may crash through again
anytime? Best to watch
the glass and gold angel that hangs
by a thread from her I.V. stand
above the bed. The angel
will bless her and you, the dead
and the living,
in that last minute –
the withering away of
body and breath –
all friends emptied from
the folded and torn map of prayer –
if I die before I wake –
by a thread.

SOMETHING ABOUT MY LIFE

When I was in high school I read Poe,
Freud, a book on Matthew's gospel, and others
on politics. None were assigned, they came
from visits to the town library. I started collecting
records of jazz greats and famous symphonies. I ran
miles and miles down the coast from Oceanside
or east out to Mission San Luis Rey, the queen
of oppression and soul saving. I was almost very good.
After the workouts which I usually did by myself,
preferred it that way, yes, all that delicious loneliness,
I went to the library to breathe and smell something
about my life. It was soon time to go to the city
bus stop at Mission and Hill Streets. I rode with
the few – young and scared – marines and their wives
or daughters back to Camp Pendleton, home for the night.
I was the only one to get off in the darkness at the road
I walked leading to the house at the top of Wire Mountain.

January 25

The wolf moon
  white teeth
  blackened gums
a howling of the eyes

I remember my father
steering the car
with so much
    grace

like the owl
gliding across
    the road
    in anticipation
    of whatever
reflection startled the light

    and how
the police helicopter circles
    tonight with its eye
    on the houses and backyards
of my neighborhood

on the human violence
    done tonight
    down the street

under the full
   wolf moon, white teeth
   gnashing and

howling until sunrise.

END RHYME

It doesn't feel like the day after Christmas
on our night flight to Dallas. Towns below
shine like clusters of stars or swirling
galaxies the names of which I'll never know.

The wings of the plane are visible in the dark,
the window reflects this page of my notebook. Take
your time in standing up for hope, you may find
yourself stung by the spider, poisoned by the snake.

This document should be retained as evidence
of your journey. Bless the ones making love
like the world will end tomorrow. Then sing
the Sanctus, lock the dead bolt, release the dove.

MY SURROUNDINGS (PART 1)

On my writing desk
is a photograph of Cora, Anna and Elleke, two
daughters, one granddaughter. Just to the right is a
photo I took of the skyline of Sarajevo
in 2003 and a postcard from a friend
with Martin Luther King's picture. Then a card sent by Anna
on Father's Day. It is entitled, "Mary and Morris Shaving"
    and refers
to the time in Montana when I taught in a two-room school.
For show and tell I got all ten kids into or near the bathroom
    and I shaved. There
was no time at home, on the ranch, to shave so I brought
    with me what I
needed. Anna was in that class, first grade and remembered
    -- so in her note on the card she wrote, "Elleke demands a
repeat performance sometime in the not too distant future
    years!" All of this
is part of what surrounds me. There is more
for another time. Tonight I am content
and filled like only a father can be filled to read
Anna's other words, "it's been so wonderful to have you
in our lives & our home & and as my dad & as Elleke's grandpa
Mike. We love you! Anna & the mini girl."
There is a lifetime here in my study, maybe just
on the desk. It is chaos until each item is looked at
and named. Does it take a clever line or phrase
to close this poem and give it the punch that makes

it more than observation or, God forbid, prose?
Then listen carefully, as I am doing, trying to return
to this past Christmas when Cora was smiling yet so sick,
Anna stood tall in her beauty and Elleke noticed the ceramic
figure on the top of a large piece of furniture and said, "fish."
Did you hear her? All of this, and more, surrounds me.

THE NOISE OF PLANTS

You walked near the
morning garden
and heard the sound
of the flowers waking
to each other, offering
coffee, a slice of toast,
a smile saying
come back to bed.
That's where it ended.
With the frown
of whatever was lost
somewhere deep
in the earth.

HOPE

It is Prague
and raining. You
speak the cold language
in the bars and on the street.
Taste this.

Hear the church
bells. They call to you
for peace, for a sober
night.

Then morning brings the lonely
quiet of the empty
sanctuary and a soft breeze
across the river, the bridge,
along the castle wall

where you stand
still waiting
with your candle.

THE DANCE

It takes so much strength
and grace
like a ballet
to stay
alive in this kitchen.
A few flowers and a box of fancy knives
on the counter with several
days of newspapers
scattered around the room as if blown
by the wind.
Then the finale, legs still,
arms moving slowly down
to the hips. The music
ends with a quiet single string
and the dance
concludes
with an arm around the neck
of one man.

SARAJEVO SYMPHONY

It's early in the evening
and I am glad. No
rush to the darkness
or a room filled
with dreams and wishes
disappearing with the
music. It is fear
and as the cello moans
like someone in quiet pain
I tuck myself between the
bed and the wall. I can hear
the morning radio news
and breathe easy again in spite
of more deaths in my daylight.
No love lost. No
love. My life is one more
humanitarian agency
pulling out because of bombs
in the plaza. Down the street
the quick response to
emergency calls suddenly
brings into question where
the bullet entered, where did
the bullet exit, when will
revenge visit this home,
whose blood is whose.

STRANGE FRUIT

(Beslan, Russia, 2004)

Here at School Number 1
you see the excitement
of the young children
on their first day. Also
the tears of parents,
their reluctance to let them
go like small apples
gently released by
the tree. They will
become ripe so very soon
as the bright red season
will come like an explosion
of color
early this fall.

SCHOOL IN SUDAN

At eight years old they took me away but taught me
    many things.
First, how to shoot the AK-47.
Then how to build a good fire and to cook for myself.
How to bury and arm land mines.
Then we were taught how to attack a village.
And then we learned how to quickly fall back.
Finally, they taught us not to think about the dead.

NOT A FAIRY TALE

The war is door to door.
You could stand only so much with
the stench of lively children
thrown into the ditch. You fill
the empty brandy glasses, keep
the shovels moving while it is still dark
and the sky is drunk with plums.

THE HOUSE

You lived just off the kitchen.
Anyone could come through
or watch what you were doing
from three different rooms. Your mind
could drift, too, into the living room
or the bathroom. The kitchen.
Your thoughts could create a meal,
an argument, or brush your hair.
Your fantasies could swirl
through the house like a magic scarf
in the wind. You could imagine
anything with wild leaps of the heart
without thought of those killing headaches.
They've been coming more often. The doctor
offers more drugs. You prefer scotch.
You prefer screaming with your eyes
at me. You prefer not expecting too much.

WEATHERED

During these
Kansas storms
I wonder what it is
like for Florence,
Loretta, Elmer,
and all the others
who have lost
those people they had
cringed with
for so many years
in dark rooms.

THE YEARS

This is the season
for the shoulders
to curve
forward. Each step
a time to gather
breath. The bad thing is
you are always looking
down and may see
a coin far,
far away.

SUNDAY'S COMIN'

-- "Walk with me, Lord"

the birds were eating
and singing
eating and singing
a meadowlark
invisible to your
eyes called to someone
in the trees
or the sky
soon the last layers
of daylight
corner you in
an orange world
where you can sing
a blue rage
in the face
of such blind silence
you pinch yourself
in disbelief

An Incident that Might
Lead to Something

BARGAINING

When my father died, I had to bargain
With his wife to obtain possession
Of his body. After several days any
Insurance would go to her in exchange
For his remains flown to California from
Wisconsin for burial at Mission Cemetery
Overlooking Mission Drive and included
Taps. I officiated. I tossed the first

Handful of dirt. Then the usual mystery masking
An investigation that could not prove murder,
Only the culmination of many domestic violence
Calls to their house as she beat up the veteran
Of two wars, Bronze Stars, wife and husband swinging
Drink, never knowing the quiet love of bringing.

TIGER

The lady is always
walking up and down
13th Street near Grove
carrying a nine iron.

She passes the Dollar Store,
Save A Lot, the Presbyterian
Church. She is on the road
back to winning.

GIVING THANKS

It was, it was,
James Brown over
my head singing in
the Podgorica hotel
by the river. As in Riga,
Tammy Wynette sang
sang from the heavens in
my favorite coffee shop. At
least these were sensible
exports from the states,
soulful art in music
not to bring me home but
to remind me of why I am gone
and to give thanks in song.
To give thanks in gravity.

VICTORY

You are dancing in your mind
    a countryside raises its voice
    to bring the silent sun

into a daytime joy. Then the rain
    of Split scatters your children
    along the coast into caves

and onto small islands of rock
    and soldiers. The dance ends
    with the banter of gun fire

we are all used to hearing. But you
    stand up, keep watch for stars
    that come victorious by the millions.

DUST TO DUST

I risk being annoying.
There is some image
in motion as my father,
in a white t-shirt, swings
at the pitched softball.
I'm sure he hit it solidly
because in this black and white
world he ran for first base
although as I risk being
annoying, maybe he missed
it by a mile. Being six
or seven I watched my
father carefully when I
could but kept a safe
distance. This must have
been a rare picnic on the base
to celebrate July 4th,
the birth of a nation, I don't
remember anything else
about the day, what kind
of food, friends my age, my
mother. Only that slow motion
shot of what I thought
was a great swing
at the ball and some dust
flying so I must have been
too close to the batter's box,
my usual dangerous risk.

fog

like a wraith
the simple ghost
of simple fear
you follow the dust,
a detective framed
by obvious clues
undeniable but such
betrayal you can
only read about
like the story of
a ship in thick
fog, deep simple fear.

EMPIRE

Across the bridge
you could see
the rustic enemy
moving in a static step
toward the town
center. The national poet
was remembered with
a statue in the square,
his face gazing,
just past the young woman
standing on the Hungarian
balcony. Everyone was still
asleep to the rhythm of summer
fans, white noise,
the blanket
covering their fear of silence.

GIVING BIRTH

You're the daughter that so surprised me
when I had you but didn't think it
was true. You're the son that still surprises
me on our phone calls, glad we see most things
the same. You're the daughter that starved so
hard you thought you were taking good care
of yourself. You're the daughter who kept
wanting out early, week by week, you finally
got your wish, remember you turning blue, grabbed
by the nurse, never to be the same.

TUNNEL

Too much purple pigment
will lead you are told
to slowly losing your
peripheral vision, that way
we have of seeing
out to the side,
right and left, making
us aware of the unexpected
disruption from a small
or large trauma
for which we pay
the rest of our lives
and it's no small cost.

VALENTINE'S DAY AGAIN

You keep thinking
up questions
with good intentions
but I am
not the one
to trust
burning tanks
and ravishing
soldiers no
matter how
many roses they bring
knocking down my door.

WHO REMEMBERS?

The bones do
and more
than that they can talk
and if you are nervous
about your past
wash your hands of it all because you will be named
as one who
should be pulled in
and made to
confess
all that you have been
and done.

VOICES

His speech was blurred
like a sad movie. It was
a surprise for such
an eloquent voice. He
was trying to be
understood through staggered
syllables
and phonetic stumbling
until finally his friends said
goodbye
which he understood
quite well.

YOUR HOPE

Your hope is in common sense.
You say your people are stupid,
not seeing what is happening or,
even worse, seeing what is not
taking place. The roses you
planted in irony have no idea
of the grammar they must work
with all across the countryside
within the structure of demanding
the bells end their ringing,
the clocks stop their clocking,
the calls to prayer go mute,
but the river still flows like justice.

JULY SUMMER

This afternoon the leaves green
with life
as opposed to envy
flail and spark in the July summer
wind, warm to the taste
as dust is to snow.

MIGHT

INNUENDO

Feet on the ground
I walk
through your aspirations
built up in my body
with undertones
of knife strikes
across the air.

There are no games
or thrones or flying
anythings today! We only
want to make
ourselves think
we are strong,
even by your suggestion.

TRUTH OR DARE

The winter is the end
and the beginning. Trees
are the escape not unlike
a small white rose
over your heart.

Would you know the truth
if it came walking
and sat down in front
of your eyes? Now
they begin tearing up

melting the vision of flames
along your spindle of rivers. If
you could just shake it off like
wool or skin, each day your memory
would seem less like the last.

INFINITY

Shhhh, let me tell you a secret.
I want to start over.
It's so much easier by myself.
Why did my friends in college
always have the perfect wife
described and in the crosshairs?
I never thought about it which
is maybe the problem. I was most
interested in surviving which is not
to be heard as a melodramatic voice.
It was the Age of Godot. Of Infinity.

ING

The water when it rains hard
Collects from one then two
Then three feet from the
Curb. Someone calls it

ponding. Does it matter?
The wording from some
Translator three countries
Away? Yes, yes it is

Important. *Laking* would
Not work nor would *seaing.*
So important that the life
Continuous, the living, the naming.

TO MAGDALENE

I have admired you from afar for years
and years. Having read about you, preached and
pictured you through two or three languages,
painting in my own flesh-strewn ways
your savvy spirit. You have inspired me
as I have drawn you in my mind like kids
with chalk on the sidewalk. Some nights
I feel you on top of me, me finally not afraid
of touch, your fingers, the curl of your legs,
the fragrance of lavender on your skin,
your ambition in our love, a strange word that
I use for your presence, the grace hard as desire
for each other ever since we were separated.
I still see you, feel your gentle weight settling me,
forever here, brave, dreaming you where you are.

THE OLD ACCUSATIVE ENDING

You brace yourself
against the tree
so you will not
fall to the ground
forever. You hold
on with all you
have, speaking words
your child would say
if she could give
you the drink of
being around when
the wind died.

THE NEWS

After hearing this
(hearing what?) he
stakes a claim on
the gravel and
stupid grass
as he stumbles
throwing rocks
favoring his left wife.

STILL LIFE

Naked ladies stand tall
in bloom and blossom,
long stems straight into
dark dirt along the road
never out of debt so you
can drink, use meth, drive
your RAM through neighboring
fields, flash a fancy belt
buckle. Now, go inside,
remove the belt swinging it
into her waiting face until
she's ground up like wheat
into flour, soy beans into
milk, love sliced like pork.
Naked ladies stand tall
in bloom and blossom,
long stems straight into
dark dirt along the road.

SPIRITUAL

Memories are safer than things
and people. Memories
are at a distance, therefore,
even at less than an arm's
length away, they are buried
and even if in a shallow grave
memories may feel the freeze.
When the truth is told what we
remember of home steals us away.

THE VOW

We are therefore given.
We are forever given.

Choices we must deny.
Choices placed before us.

Like the caul covering us.
Like the veil therefore given.

To keep us from drowning.
In our own birthing mess.

SLEEP

As the spiral deepens
you want most of all
to move toward bed
as soon after dinner
as possible, or credibly
polite and genuine. It feels
like you are rushing away
from the crowd of family,
even if only the two of you
but darkness drags its
beautiful, bulging feet as
you crawl into the bathroom,
find the help you need and
in slow motion you brush
your teeth, comb out your
hair, look to see if anyone is
watching, then you wait under
the covers for the first induced
yawn, thank god for pills and water.

GARDEN

If it blooms
it's a flower.
You never weed
the garden
because it is all
unknown and
beautiful. Besides,
what have those
wild plants
done to you?

SHHHHH (Yes, again)

> *But despite how many of us were in the bed,*
> *I felt alone.* - Kristen Dombeck

Let me tell you a secret.
I want to start over. *Shhhhh.*
It's so much easier by myself.
Why did my friends in college
always have the perfect spouse
described and in the crosshairs?
I never thought about it which
Is maybe the problem. I was most
Interested in surviving which is not
to be seen as melodrama. It was
the Age of Godot. Of Infinity.

PROFILING

The face in the mirror
is spare and local,
looking like a small
flower, a tiny
black blossom.

As this flower,
known as *other*, shuts
the door behind her,
walks out into the
caved world, who will notice

the lively spirit, the love
of the neighborhood
air and sky? She takes strong,
long strides leading her
to the end, no going back.

IN TRIBUTE

Please read Ellen Bass's poem, "The Kitchen Counter,"
For a familiar feeling we all have or will before
You know it. Imagine sliding or slithering across the tiles
Almost to the sink, holding on to a cabinet door
As the rhythm of new life is breathed into you
And that's not all. Closing your legs around
Those hips, your thighs shining and strong
As the day you won the race. You keep living your
Strength as beautiful sweat runs like rain
Along your high cheek bones, you tumble along
And that's not all as deep inside there are two voices
In your one throat, begging for more juice,
Hugging some frightful burden, more and more
Giving in to sweet disguised as salt, and everything.

DAY TO DAY

Cory Lewandowski is not
The person I wish to spend
The morning with so I change
The channel and am face
To face with Jared Kushner.
Now my anxiety is reaching
Beyond the caffeine and political
Treason that seems so obvious
But so complex. Our world has
Wars, thirty-eight dead in Kabul
Today but getting no air time.
Healthcare is another case of
Stupidity turning to lethal
Behavior. The *options* are killing us.
And the wealthy are not sent
Empty away.

LEAD

BLIND MAN

The twist and spin of the dancer in your dream
Gives you a pleasant turn, round and round until
The beginning becomes the end. The turn in the
Road traces the tires along the yellow line
Back to the dented ego nothing could destroy,
Sweet is the fragile air of lilac, the sanctuary
For your heart, too bad it wasn't around when you
Were five although I don't think they grow in Maine,
Only where there is more than a glimpse of summer
Like here, the great American desert filled with irrigation
Wells, heard a blind man say, there goes a sight for my
    sore eyes.

AS THE PAIN SETTLES

I.

Was it you I asked
about? Wanted to
know your symptoms
and where the pain
had settled? If you need
anything like narcotics
or massage therapy, please
let me know. The world
is so much, I will do
what I can, my best.

II.

The world is so heavy.
I wake up bent over
but manage to shake off
my locked bones and brain
fog in an hour or two.
Then I open my body to
the world, look for the
proper caption for my
photo and face another
crush or two. My body.
This world has symptoms
no body or bottle can
fix. I hope you will
understand as I have
to protect my body
from being taken.

AGAINST

the tide and the waves you gamble
your life for one. Then you must decide
the words to write in the sand, a message
to back your actions. When you face north
imagining freedom, eyes watering and still
no words come with the cold red of your
skin. Stripped to nothing you are not one to
feel shame so this is new. And it's forever.

TILL THE LAST DOG IS HUNG

Really? That's the way
It goes? Yes, but we don't know how it started, where
It came from. Those specific
Words are ugly although
Some people laugh out of
Wonder or disbelief, I know
I often laugh during my
Knowing years for the same
Reasons. What about you?
Is there any wonder or
Disbelief causing you to laugh?

ELEGY FOR NOW

He had that edge of panic on his voice.
The wet air was rising off the ground.
Although no one heard the paper to fire,
we all stood around making our choice

for a wedding night's loss. The pillow
gained strength but the two of you did not.
Soon your face will sleep like a child's hand.
Burn the entire village while you say no

to living like a blur across the sky.
Think of the holidays and all the children
scattered around the country because of your
shattered dream only able to say - let me die.

CLASS INTRODUCTION

I am from here, Mostar.
I have two pets,
a cat and a bunny
but I can't give
them names. If I do
I will get too close
to them, have many
feelings for them. I may
come home some day
and my mom will have
done something with them.
I hide them in my
bedroom. This is one
of the things in my life.

CLEVELAND

I bet the spider's greatest fear
is the shoe. Mine's being kidnapped.
My mother can watch
The Walking Dead while she eats dinner.
London is north of Cleveland and we
explode into a heated argument
about geography, map making
and our greatest phobias. It turns out
he is also very afraid of the shoe
as he orders me into the car, covers
my eyes and I know then my
greatest fear is being realized.

DANTE'S HOUSE, FLORENCE

When in the rain - - -
The dark train - - -
When in the rain - - -
The dark train - - -

We descend into
Or ascend into
The glory of the suffering Jesus
In hundreds and hundreds of churches
In this city but nothing
Saves like the sweet and holy
Water of Beatrice's tears washing
My recently dead
Long white body.

DIOCLETIAN'S ROOM, SPLIT, CROATIA

I have heard this is the largest
Or only fish market without flies!
Because, you may want to know,
There is a large small medium size
Batch of sulfur nearby. And in one of the squares
There is a statue of Croatia's most
Famous literary person, I can't
Remember his name. This afternoon
I parked the rented Opel from Mostar and we walked
Down toward the *Riva,* passing beautiful
Women, a wedding, stone older than most gods,
Tall handsome men, kids and their dads playing soccer
In St. Mark's Square. Then the water,
Wide open spaces, a church, kava,
And the Adriatic beyond the islands. It was all
Ideal until walking back, tired and lost
We asked for directions which were ideal
Until we reached the place where I had parked
The black Opel in front of a sign that apparently read,
For mothers with child and the handicapped only.
Because we ran into so many helpful people including
The young women in the clothing shop saying it happens
To them about once a month, Peter the taxi driver who knew
Verona, the owner of a small apartment, we got to the police
Impoundment center, retrieved the Opel and followed
Peter back to the Old Town of Split where we had our
    ideal time,

Thanks to Verona and the off-season priced apartment
In the walls of Diocletians's retirement palace.
Soon I was falling asleep in his room, really,
Surrounded by cold stone walls three feet thick
And warm people, now no longer invisible, in a world,
I heard that is not as complicated as the one east of here,
Across the mountains, the country shaped like the live
    human heart.

THE COLOSSEUM, ROME

If you have never been to Rome,
Italy, and many have not,
just to warn you it is a city
of *details*. Every place you look,
every corner you turn, there will be
the drama of a huge recycled
(renaissance)
building or monument or maybe
both and the same. Leaving Rome,
on the train to Florence, the
pain wants to eat its own bone,
a self-gladiating wish for freedom.

THE PRINCESS AND THE FROG
-For Adi

At the top of a high hill
In Skopje
We walked toward
The shrine honoring Katerina,
Later to be named Emina
After she converted.

There were green dollar signs
And other graffiti on the columns
As well as *Amir + Selma* and other
Names and comments
Spray painted or crassly carved
On this holy place.

We learned that students used
To come to the shrine, place their
School books and written work
On the stone floor, shielded by the curved
Dome
Overhead supported by the four

Stone, disfigured columns. The students
Were hoping for a special
Blessing on their work
And desperate for the best
Grades in spite of poor performance.

On the walk back up the path, away

From the shrine we spotted a used

Condom, cast off among the ancient gravel stones.

Someone had found another way, some soft curves and
kisses

Worth extra sweat and hard breath in this

Thin air, witnessed by the shrine

Itself and the most sacred of ancient gods.

ITALY

I can't get
to where
I am.
This is us.
Go with the
flaw is a
clothing ad
in Rome.
I couldn't
say it better.

MOSTAR WALK AFTER THE WAR

Walking the afternoon streets
Quiet on a Sunday shadows
Long across the new buildings
And those still with shrapnel marks
And missing walls. There is one
With the second floor shredded
Open to see the bathroom tile
Exposed and the pipes hanging while
They catch their breath at the sight
Of nephews slaughtered in the bright.

UMAMI

Your skin
reminds me
of the l-
glutamates,
a savory
meat flavor
approaching
a national
dish,
specialty
of the house,
and I imagine
your kiss.

NEO-NATAL

One of the graves appears
In my dream.

It is the same year
As the others.

1993.*

A hand moves in front of my eyes
And slowly is joined by another to

Stroke my cheek, as if to be kind.
But nothing is ever as it seems here

So I am lulled into comfort and caring
When a knife blade is set against my

Throat. The pressure increases as one layer
Of skin is pierced.

The grave in my dream slowly
Falls into its self.

A dog begins to bark, someone
Yells at it to shut up.

It's strange to hear English for anything
Spoken near me.

It is also unusual to feel those hands
Still gentle with my face, as if I was just born.

*1993 A particularly brutal year in Mostar during the
Bosnian war.

PAINTINGS ON THE WALL

It seems like
a lazy dance
of loving
turned inside out
like a blouse
backward-armed
impossible to put on
in a morning rush
or the lost cave
you wandered into
your last night here
while everyone laughed
at your historic paintings
on the wall.

KRV

-Bosnian for "blood"

Take the garden into the back yard and the fruit
Trees, harvest them so we can make (pies) and sell the
   honey
On the street for whatever people can pay, if anything,
Don't push them, don't corner them, we are facing a new
Day each day as the mountains move, as the sweat soaks
Through my shirt, as the movie ended but we don't know
   how.

LAUGHTER

The comedy of the storm
rolled in its own laughter
up the Neretva River,
lightning slamming into
the large rocks along the
bank of blue. The strike
like on a prairie haystack
exploded into fire. The city
fought back and to this day
the legend is told: We live.

MASS, SAN CARLO CHURCH, FLORENCE

Because I was listening
to the longest homily in the
liturgical history of
Catholicism and was tired
from walking for days around
a beautifully overwhelming city
of art, religion and politics,
it was an act of keeping
myself awake to
notice on the wall
behind the communion
table a large
painting of the dead
Jesus being prepared
for burial by eight
or ten people, mostly
women, all but one
covered. Jesus is naked
with no male genitals
where they should be
and more than the beginnings
of breasts where they should be.
I wonder if the model
for Jesus was really female or is there
perhaps another explanation?

PRESENT CONTINUOUS

(For Ramo and my 4th year BiH students)

We, we
know the worst
but don't
know how
to say it.

We, we
can't tell
even the
present form
of the past.

We, we
know the best
but don't
know how
to say it.

We, we
can't tell
even the
present form
of the future.

SOMETHING

WATCHING NETFLIX IN HERZEGOVINA

(CRNA KOMEDIJA)

It's a program, a mystery,
set in Iceland as our
current project. Called, "Trapped,"
the first episode finds a
human torso floating in the sea,
pulled out frozen by police – I guess
a naked human torso floating in the sea
next to Iceland would be frozen, *duh*
as my grand daughter would say. And
to add to the plot of snow and ice
the police take the torso to the largest
freezer – except outdoors – around which is
the fish company, of course. A Lithuanian,
of course, guy recently off a docked ferry
has two young Nigerian girls with him in a Chevy
1970's camper since it is Iceland and he is
involved with child slavery and the Baltic
mob. He gets stuck in the deep snow,
runs away but is caught on foot in the dark while the two
Nigerian girls escape the camper and disappear
into a blizzard wearing just one layer
of clothing. End of Episode One. 51 minutes.

MOSTAR MORNING

I like the light,
lift the metal shades
on the outside of the window
of our apartment. I pull
the ingenious strap
from the inside
as the shades slide together
and rise out of sight
above the window like
the sun rising in time
lapse. Below are
the customers at a café
some of them my students
drinking coffee and kissing
for breakfast. English
literary terms don't
sink in but float
on the surface like
the ducks on the Neretva.
Lovers and light both gaze
through my window shining,
again, like the sun and the
magnifying glass of
my childhood, burning a hole
through my butterfly wing.

FAKE SKELETON WITH HAT

It was worth a try.
Maybe he was constantly
Late for work. Or perhaps
He was a practitioner
Of comedy, or, given his
Passenger, tragedy. He is one
Of 7,000 a year who illegally
Use the HOV lane in Arizona.

He was spotted by the authorities
Who saw the strange companion.
First, the hat, then the skull
Under the hat. The offender was
Only wanting to be in the fast lane,
Only wanting to be on time, finally.

YOU WANTED AN ACCESSIBLE POEM

The moon and midnight
swarm over the many
graves of all the people
I buried during my
career. I use these
ordinary words for
those of you wishing
to read an accessible
poem from me. I hope
the three of you are happy
and know all that comes
next. The moon and midnight
swarm over the many graves
of all the people I burned
during my tired love and rage,
do not go into that night, gently.

ROBIN WILLIAMS

In the five months after
Robin Williams killed himself,
the suicide rate in the U.S. increased
by 10%. Living here in Mostar
the view of the horizon is often
murky but I can at least breathe. Why?
Others who live here raise bees
or sheep on small farms –
bled for the real world long
after the BBC left. Now, the case
against the criminals in court
makes news even back in the states
because of a court room suicide.
Why?

IN THE HAMMOCK AT JOEL AND
TRACY'S PLACE AUSTIN, TX
- *After James Wright*

I don't know why but I was
able to fall asleep in the blink of a heartbeat.
In the air between two trees.

It was a new thing
to be able to drop off as soon as
my eyes were closed. This time I was wearing
one of several baseball caps Joel gave me
as a son does for his father
to keep the light off the skin.

This time he also put his baby daughter,
Luisa, on my chest but I did not feel her slight weight
as we both floated
in the air between two trees.

She noticed before I did. I tried to calm her
but she took a look at me so close, face to face, and
     screamed
the birds out of the trees, tried to wiggle off into outer
     space
but her dad was right there for her
as his dad was not, water
seizing the bridge, over, under, washed out

and down to the Clearwater. Shortly after the
     hammock visit
I found out why sleep came so easily. Quietly an

obsession
    of cells
formed a lump, an obsession of cells
in the air between two trees.

NOT HOMER (SIMPSON)

She arched her back
to find God
or a version,
the first edition,
of the Epic
sea-voyage,
avoiding the hidden
shoreline of rocks
and the rip tide.

MY COUNTRY

Your hope is in common sense.
You say your people are stupid,
not seeing what is happening or,
even worse, seeing what is not
taking place. The roses you
planted in irony have no idea
of the grammar they must work
with all across the countryside
within the structure of demanding
the bells stop ringing and the calls
to prayer end and the green river,
the blue river, must it dry up like me?

THE TREE

A skinny tree comes into view
Plodding along on a very distant
Handmade pathway. Too much
Of that world is in this world.
I imagine everyone wearing two
Sets of clothes, pajamas for sleep
And the work clothes worn over them
Since there is only sleep and work,
Sleep and work. Today I read
A poem by Nye where she uses
even-ing, and the *resonance of moor*
On the Isle of Mull, Scotland.
Because we worry about friends
Back on the North Sea coast of
Scotland, it matters, all that salt
Tide and the black-ing of rock.

'GATOR DINER

Here in central Florida
the green and white
sign directs you to
a green and white building
for dinner. Now, finally,
something to believe in
because up to this moment
nothing is trusted, no one
is telling me the truth. You
can keep quiet about
the stuff that happened
thinking it won't be
stirred all up again but
you can be very sure
it is always there, always
here, always smiling like
a lie whispered in your sleep.

AID AND COMFORT

GAZA 2012

The sweet apricots spoil
on the ground. The neighbor
rooster crows as the call
to prayer begins at 4
a.m. just outside the plastic
covered window. The songs
merge in the dust and smoke of
anything that will burn. The survival
hotel has its own chickens
for omelets to serve
the few of us allowed
here to attempt aid
and comfort. I listen to thin
children for hours tell me about
seeing their families slaughtered
by silence while the world
whispered among its own
like paper money slipping
through their fat fingers.

A SMALL HARD STONE

GAZA 2012

They said I was tiny and tough
even when I was born. Some people
still say the same. I go to the
roof of our Gaza home to read
the stars and to talk to my
husband. He always said when
he died, go to the roof of our house
and talk to me.

What do I do now that there
is no house, only a scar on the
ground. If I am tiny and tough
I should knock down all the walls.
I should listen to the tiny and tough
girl inside me then do what she says.

Soon it will be over. We cannot
judge one another, only be tough
and tiny, shrinking away into a small hard stone.

I NOTICE HER

carrying an edge,
not like a cliff
or a canyon,
closer to a knife
but dull
leaving a wound
ragged as
snake skin
and steaming
like winter's breath.

SOLITARY CONFINEMENT

You don't have to do what they say.
Find your own way through the
demands and expectations of every
phone call or sexy move. The
daylight is more convenient for those of
you who wish a more visible truth. During
the dark you can solve or disrupt
the life of anyone's dreams. You can
offer this access to art that most
will not feel but only disregard.
Or you can feed on the brain-cleansing
spices that make memory more of a clear
domain rich in life experience, and
beach memories and full pages of solitary
confinement. You will find that even
when the war inside you breaks loose
your truth will be a casualty soon,
if not the first. Then you will seek
some negotiation for peace, for an end
to unquiet losses, something to make you smile.

SEVDAH

Of
all things

I never
thought

my heart
would

be
the problem.

You Must Have Your Famine

WHERE ARE MY CHILDREN?

"IF THIS ENDS"

If this ends   will we
   still be friends (question)

Probably not (answer)   That makes me sad (statement)

Why (question)   I will miss you (answer)

It will be impossible (statement)   Why (question)

It will be too painful (answer)   For you (question)

No, for you (answer)

MISSING

Where are my children?
They were with me
when we all
went to sleep at dark
last night. I've been
going mad for years
in fear this kind of thing
would happen.

But what is "this kind of thing"?
Any minute now
I will lean out this window
of my apartment
and scream for the five of them:
Listen. You were with me at dark.

WAITING, WANTING,

Waiting, wanting,
standing, storming.
The pain
has been strong
since coming back
from the bridge.
This is
not an apology.
I am one
of the last
to use film,
even black and white.
On the bridge
I decided
just a few
more photos.

SANTA MONICA

We could not
Stand each other
For one more meal
Or television show,
Another sweet smile
Smothered in gravy
Or traffic jam
The length of 10
From Santa Monica
To wherever it finally
Finds allelulla freedom,
Which, as Janis Joplin
Reminded us, is just
Another word for
Nothing else to lose.

RETURN FLIGHT

baby, it's cold
outside
i know
you really
must go
i just want
to say
we should try
one more
time
time
is with us
we can keep
warm
warm
is with us
more time
more time
more time
round trip

MARRIAGE

Walking the river
With the wind coming
From the usual south
The ripples of surface
Water go the way
Of the wind – disguised
As rushing north.
But the deep wellship
Of the river flow
Is moving otherwise
In opposition to
The blind world so
Angry at the filthy
Truth that sets
The river free
To flood at will.

LOVER

The fabric tulip
keeps its shape
long into the
winter. I do
well remember
holding your face
in my hands
gentle as a lover
and I so well
remember your
soft line of
skin along the
cheek bone on each
side of your face.
Believe me, when I
say, you were the only
one? I know of
your skeptic nature,
full embrace coming
so absent of abandon.

YOUNG BRIDE

The bride, so young,
in her white dress,
could not speak
but only squealed
nervous laughter
as we gathered at the
front of the sanctuary.
This was her day
between the high notes
of her musical fear
when the taking of a
breath brought silence.
She prayed for hope
that the sacred vow
would break through
the terror of losing
it all, her whole life,
to a handsome violence
that would make her
scream and twist
until her last laugh
and her final breath
forced blood stains
on that white dress.

LAST KISS

I remember Karen Lynch.
But I probably should not use her
Name like this in public. Wait!
This is a poem, no one in the public domain
Will read it so her name won't become an instant
Household word. There's no fear of libel.
Like I was saying, I remember Karen Lynch.
Nineth grade. Kansas. She was beautiful,
Too beautiful for me. Me, too shy for her.

What I don't remember is how I was talked
Into asking her to the movies, or how
I got up the courage to put my arm
Over her shoulders in the dark of the back row,
Or how we turned to each other
At the exact same moment, accidentally
Brushing our lips softly together, like a
southern summer breeze that, all of a sudden,
Turns from the north signaling violence.

FLOOR

There is often
that tension over
speaking or not
when you are half over
me and covering my
face with
kisses. We are trying
to recover something in
our lives. And as with
many people it is
awkward. I feel a dull
ache in the pelvic floor –
like an open mouth
wanting to scream
but failing. I remember
now the untangling
of our legs
and arms, a clumsy
caress of my breast,
or maybe it was my face.
And I know you recall
how we stood carefully,
not looking into
each other's eyes,
we embraced
as one ex to another.

BODY UNIDENTIFIED

You drift closer to
the mainland. Low
flying airplanes and
boats of various sizes
search from the sky
and the surface spotting
illusions of hope for
your life. Nameless
you float with the
ebb of the tide and
the pull of the moon.
You are a creature
of the sea having made
a lifetime for the
world's survivors to
search out. Even if
discovered the naming
will be impossible
as no one will dare come
forward to claim you.

THE POND AND THE TEAL

The pond has a heart
And it throbs loud
And steady for the teal.
It is July and years
Since the breaking up
Of a love lyric with
Smiles anyone passing by
Would recognize as fragile
Like the gold leaf around us.
The teal and the pond are
Beautiful in this photo
Taken around the same time
As they fantasized a life together.

PLAYING IT SAFE

Out of the corner of your eye
You see an ad on television
For a video game. All you see
Are the words: Play your heart out.
But you are already
Standing on the edge
With little heart left
For more risk-taking.
You have asked your
Therapist about some way
To put your heart in a cast
To help the healing. She replies,
It is not a bone, how would
It work? You reply, You are wrong,
My heart is bone, not flesh, not
A muscle, therefore it does
Not tear, it breaks.
And it is a compound fracture.
So, please, wrap it in cloth
And plaster, let it dry.
Someone may want to sign their name.

DYING FOR LOVE

Does he talk about
what he believes?
No. Just wanting
the angels to come
and take him. Sounds
like belief to me. Yes?
I'm told you can
make money with aloe plants.
You have to find the right
people to buy them.
The bigger the plant
the more buyers will spend.
Do they believe in the healing?
Whether angels or aloe
we come to the same
desert expanding on its own
and changing the nature
of the beautiful continent.
Dust becomes us and
the earth tumbles into
the lush green of our
love. Pulling the sheets up
over us we can laugh
and be buried at the same time.

AMICABLE

There was this road
traveling the river.
Sooner, rather than later,
they argued. Even the
tallest of the old trees
trembled as the raging
continued. Winter after
winter, season from season,
the road and the river
threw bad names and
rocks at each other.
I remember this as a
child. I am still haunted
by the sight of empty
stream beds, small trees
terrified to grow to fullness,
and even what were the high
grasses stunted by neglect
and hate. I witnessed this
death and you were
with me. We both starved
and, even in our anger, we
could not destroy each other.

FIRST KISS

Often during the night
I hear only the sound
of the neighbor's television.
The words all run
together, melting into
one long monologue
of chatter with a
scream or a shout
to occasionally interrupt
the drivel. Now, there's a word
we don't see every day!
It's like a discovery for
this special moment. Like
moving my hand up a
very smooth and naked
leg, the first kiss of
love-falling, during the night,
often, I hear only the sound.

LOOSE CHANGE

We met for coffee
at a large bookstore.
I was standing in front
of the Lonely Planet guides
when you came up behind me.
I felt the light touch
of your breasts through
your blouse and my shirt
against my back and your face
resting on the pillow
between my shoulder blades.
I know your smile
gave the security
cameras something to talk about
when they finished
their shift and went wherever
security cameras go
for rest and a good meal.
Then you slipped your hands
into my front pants pockets.
You were not searching
for nickels or dimes.

THE SPIDER

You make it sound so easy.
Then you change your mind
And bring the argument into
Focus from a different
Angle. You don't notice
The black spider walking
Along the edge of your
Coffee cup. The discussion
Continues – mostly on
The literary merits of a full
Stop. But you forget about
The war around us,
The anger and fear
Striking like lightning
Ourselves and our neighbors.
The world knows nothing,
Cares less. You could
Put your hands gently
On the side of my face
Only for the sake of affection.
The spider is oblivious,
Spins a web across your cup.

TIGER, TIGER

What is intimate to you
Is only what gets caught
In your teeth. It takes
Practice to do what you do
With such skill. The play
With siblings in childhood,
Faking a throat-grab then
A sharp snap at the rump
Is only a prelude to the love
Of the kill that will come
Sooner than I ever imagined.
You're down on your stomach
In the brown grass with more
Patience than you can keep
Hidden. You move toward your
Prey before your instinct would
Allow so you know it's a mistake
From the start. I see what
You are doing so I lunge
Out of the reach of your
Lecherous, poor-excuse-for-claws
Attack and you tumble away
Out of view, over the steep cliff,
Dropping out the window on the
Twentieth floor and land on
The pavement, the sweet savanna
Twisted and contorted in more
Erotic ways than you can picture
On the pavement, the sweet savanna.

EVENING NEWS

It was a blood moon
but the news reporter
said: "Blue moon." She
never corrected herself.
This Tuesday was a beautiful
spring day but the
news reporter cautioned
us, saying, there are
reports of possible severe
storms from the
southwest. She continued
with how cool dry air
would or 'could' meet with
warm moist air
right over our state.
Stay tuned, she warned.
I considered the Percocet
left over from a recent
hospital visit. There is an
enjoyable high from the
narcotic but also the usual
caution about addiction and,
since that runs in my
family, I decided to heed
the warning. I waited for
the next blue moon, severe storms.
I am staying tuned in.

WINTER FORECAST

The newspaper forecast
is for a lot of snow
this year. It would be
unusual in this part of
the Great Plains. I could
be expected to dream
about the ice you
have melted with your
body near mine. It is
a life-saving trick
when stranded by a
blizzard. Take off our
clothes, each of us,
crawl into the sleeping bag
skin to skin. If we are lucky
the body warmth will help
us survive the coldest night.

HARVEST

We have to do something
With the tomatoes. It was
Thirty-seven degrees last night.
The image falls on the retina,
For her – a membrane of despair.
We have to do something.
She cannot keep holding her knees
Up to her head and feel comforted.
It is time for the harvest,
Salvage everything now or nothing
Will get us through the winter.
Even the slope of the roof looks
Unprepared for the snow to come.
The whole house looks sad
And frightened by the coming
Weather. The dogs already
Are spending nights in the haystacks
Building their bodies with warm
Blood while they have nightmares,
Barking and whining in their sleep.

THE NEW

The new moon, meaning
No moon that I can see,
Could be blood red or yellow
As dying leaves. Come and go
Radiating or in silence
With your body across mine
I imagine, remember, the bombing
Of the city and waiting for so much
To happen in our lives
And waiting and waiting
Finally gathering it all with us
For that one year of care,
Caress and love the color
Of leaves or the moon bleeding.

WILLOW WEEP

as you always do no matter
what the occasion, magnitude,
or tiny sad delay in our lives.
Still you have that same chronic
stoop of the shoulders while your
many limbs drag along the sidewalk,
wave with the breeze to the sway
of history. On this date in 1812
Beethoven wrote a passionate letter
to an unknown woman. Don't we all?

THE OTHER WOMAN

You would be hard to explain.
You come in and stand, walk around,
in and out the door. You go to the
playground.

Be careful. Watch your step. You go to the swing.
Up and back, into the air. You try to fly out of the way.

PANSION STARI GRAD

Juliet, Juliet, that is the hurting part.
You wake up
and in the mirror
see your life
only
in black and white.
Juliet, that is the hurting part.
It's a life-threatening situation for those of you
living north of Paradise, praying in Nebraska. Juliet
open your eyes
as you wake up
see yourself
in black and white.
Your life
depends on it, north of Paradise, the hurting part.
Juliet, Juliet,
and it's grown to be
a life-threatening situation for
those of you under siege in Stari Grad, across the
ocean
from Paradise, that is the hurting part,
open your eyes, see the blackbirds, thirteen
of them only in black and black
you wake up.
Your life depends

on it, the situation

threatening Paradise,

Juliet, Juliet, you are

not invited to the party, open your eyes to the life-

threatening possibilities north of Paradise.

Juliet, Juliet, that is the hurting part.

SCOTTISH PRAYER BOOK

HISTORY OF SCOTLAND

You walk along the beach
with the angled stones,
huge flat rocks, sliding
out of the water and sand
but not moving, dead still.
You balance from one ancient
massive miracle to another
daring any one of them to
throw you into the water but
you are conquering all of
nature and your own worry
about leaving the beach
and going back to the house.
The danger in small rooms
shows on your salted face.
Your tight fist, another
example of a geological
work of god, also the size
of your pounding heart,
also the only way to
make your life a choice
fighting through the muir,
the moor, the Scottish history
of never quite breaking away
in spite of spears, drums and
pipes. Cold sea water offers
the escape of drifting away.

CUPID AT THE NORTH SEA

I am leaning toward giving up.
Perhaps it's hormones or just
Getting older, losing confidence
Or interest. No, not losing interest.
There are times when I feel the wave
Of desire and I am encouraged. I see
Someone's smile to me and mine to her.
Someone's smile to me and mine to her.

I recently read an article in the AARP
Magazine about Cher: She says:
"I'm not stepping aside, yet." But I
Am not Cher. And I am not dead!
I'll continue to enjoy those smiles and
The wave of desire with its sea salt taste.

TRAIN TO EDINBURGH

Scotland, 2014

Our next stop is Dundee.
It is a point of change
For many going to Glasgow
Or other towns surrounded
By sheep and bales of hay.
You sit across the aisle,
Facing each other, the table
Between you. You face
Opposite directions. One of you
Reads but you look out
The window as if praying
Or planning. You're walking
The beach across from Fife
Holding hands, kissing the bite
Of her lips, crazy in love.
You glance at the sky,
Catch your breath in the surprise
Of love-making reflected
In the window of the train.
Holding you close, she
Asks you not to cry in front
Of everyone. She says,
Catch your breath, and read.

AUBADE

It's French for dawn so start
with a bright morning.
Uncover your head to the sky
and clear the fight
from your eyes. Bless the
small flowers under your bare
feet and wash from your memory
the tides of St. Monan's.
Fire is in the stove, the black
dirt will swell the seed
to growth for a second cutting.
Tears are too wet to help
and the salt will dry white on your
boiled face eyeing the sea.

MY BEAUTIFUL PUB

The ale has every intention
Of frothing over the lip
For a chance
To have her fingers
Caress the foam
And the glass.
She reads the language
Of the grasses
Coming out of the Borders.
Night in the valley
Gives way to
The blues playing
In the only coffee shop
Among the few
Homes left living
The seclusion
Along the shallow
River Tweed.
Even the clouds
Cannot keep
Their secrets knowing
She is watching the sky
With the black of her eyes.

BBC ALBA

The dark place of the past
two weeks has been choking
you like the brogue or brick
on the coast near Cullen.
The farther north we come
the more solid the call for
independence . That is why I
came here, as close to the rock
edge as I've been in years.
Now feel how much is love, how
much is cleaning up the mess.

LEAVING HEATHROW

We begin to fly over
the North Atlantic
and immediately
encounter turbulence
which halts
the beverage service.

I fall asleep
imagining the disappearance
of my pension
and Social Security.
I don't like political dreams.
I fall from grace, actually
I jump. It is a slow
decline like the decent
into Chicago. I have been
cleared to land
and disguise my dreams.
More turbulence.

DUNNOTTAR CASTLE, STONEHAVEN, ABERDEENSHIRE

Fate is sealed with the North Sea
On one side and Cromwell's army
On the other – there is more to this
Than meets the eye – the "aye" –
Yes! And a double Scotch to calm
The nerves of combat. Take
The crown jewels for instance,
No, really, take them and
Hide them so they
Disappear for decades.
Maybe someone will find
Them in a trunk or something.
There is more than meets
The eye. Yes! Look into mine.
I have not felt this way
In decades. I want
To laugh. I want to believe
There is hope, like the tide
Filling the harbor forever.

BEGGAR'S BELIEF

*

The roads are wet with the October rain
and I walk. Keep walking. The sea to the north ends
in ice. In ancient stories, the gods send storms from
the north.
"This crazy weather," they say here in Moray,
"wait five minutes and it will change."
I hear the same in Kansas.

*

I have not written much about you
so I will be direct: You were my nephew,
my sister's son, sent to me by our mother when you
were eight.
She hoped I would calm the storm already stirring
inside you, put you on the magical yellow brick
road leading to the Emerald City.
Instead you stole auto repair tools from
the hardware store next door
hoping to take them back home to California
to please your dad. That would be
for you, the Emerald City, to give
your dad something he needed
and he would be glad, and he would
hug you and say, Evan, I love you.

*

I could only find you a not-so-magical
dirt road. You discover all the rents,
stones and ragged-edged holes
and you fell head first.

*

The call came from your stepdad.
Your girl friend returned the ring.
Standing in the restaurant parking lot
you put the .45 to your head, the one in your dad's
truck, his gun, at twenty-four.

It's a dirt road
around your whole body.
Head first.

*

The storm waves crash on the rocks
washing your feet. The wind is being
it's stormy self, still angry at you.
Interesting that your name means rock.
You have anchored yourself at the edge of the world,
standing tall, you beg the arctic ice
to come closer

because now you believe, ashes and all.

GORILLA COFFEE

Looking across Princes Street
I see the contemporary art
Building and above it,
Edinburgh Castle.

Wars rage, ISIS threatens
The world, my wife is
Buying a few clothes
To replace the ones

In her lost luggage.
"25 Years of Contemporary
Art in Scotland," features
The Art of Golf.

I will not go there.
But I will finish
My coffee called:
Gorilla Coffee. Beans

From Rwandan farmers
To help lift them out
Of poverty. A family laughs.
They are not from Rwanda.

CULLEN SKINK

One morning, my Texas
granddaughter, on her way
to first grade observed:
"Rules are…
unattractive."

I recall this as I walk
down North High Street,
Portsoy, Banffshire,
wishing she was with me.
We would meet many

dogs and people would
let us walk their dogs
like we did in Austin
last July. Luisa!!
Your name would be

a good one for Scotland
although it's a long way
from home here at the edge
of the world. But I know
you would understand

you do not have to taste
my bowl of skink, you can choose
macaroni and cheese instead.
It would also help if you would hold
my hand as my world becomes
less and less like yours.

SCOTTISH SONNET

Each day is different.
I have to spend time here
Close to the sea stacks
Of red and black sandstone
Moving into and out of
The quiet North Sea imagining
A tide. Fool the life
Of all identity.

Waves carry the spirit
From me to you over
The years, the miles.
It costs so much,
"it" being what is given
In the stone and the buried.

AFFECTION

On the train to Aberdeen
The young woman, travelling
With her boyfriend, was
Reading a book: I LOVE DICK.
The young man was also reading
But I could only see a part
Of the cover. It was an American
Flag but instead of stars in the blue
There were small Nazi symbols.
I wanted to talk, discuss
The books but in the midst of their reading
They were being very affectionate
With each other. I did not want
To bother them. A small table
Separated us so it was difficult
Not to watch their enjoyment
Of each other. I tried to bury myself
In my own book by Lahiri: THE LOWLAND.
Subhash and Holly were just getting
To know each other. He began
Staying at her small house when
Her son, Joshua, stayed the weekend
With his father. I read about
Their enjoyment of each other.

FIBER

I expected you would say that.
Not because I am psychic
But only watching as the North Sea
Pounds the brains of this planet
With wisdom and we do not
Embrace the love of salt
And muscle. We hand over
The fiber of our souls
To some insane, lost god,
Without the faintest hope
Of gathering the battered
Night-sound of seedlings
Betrayed by the very soil
Meant to be our home.

ORKNEY'S

You have your teeth
Back and it feels so much
Better. You return to
Tearing apart your
Rare beef steak
And pound the table
With guttural abandon.
The little ones watch
With no worry
For their own lives
As long as you remain
Where you are with teeth
Locked into muscle
And flesh like the iron
Jaws of the trap
Sprung in time, just
In time, to save
John Groat from the
Imprisoned faces of grief,
Island to island.

TAKE YOUR SCOTTISH LIFE

Stand close to the ocean home.

You can close your right hand into a fist.

Love the waves breaking over your out-stretched arm.

You are the only one who goes this far into the North Sea.

That is not true. Others go to great lengths

To take their lives far out to sea,

Drop them like an anchor.

SCOTTISH SONNET #8 (CROVIE)

If we had a king size bed
We could go all day and night
Without touching each other.
It would be the size of a country,
Twice as large as a desert.
I've been told I can be annoying.
Spare the change and bring me the rest
Before nightfall. I have friends

In low places I never knew about.
They will watch over me and not just
This one time but forever or as long as I live.
From this high up you can see all the houses
I stormed out of, the waves so strong I'll never
Ever dare again to trouble the waters.

"LADE"

(Scot's for: channel of water)

I suppose I've mentioned
wanting to see your horses
because I want to see you.

And perhaps I asked about
your daughter because I like
to see your face when you speak

of her. She has so much courage,
you say. I say, I believe she
got that trait from you. I linger

at the door convinced of the safety
of being near you and talking.
Sometimes you have put your

hand on my arm before I open
the door to leave. Always, I hope
for my own courage until next time.

THE CLIFFS OF MOHER

Ireland, 2014

It's a long drop to the sea
Or an impossible climb to the top.
The county is Clare and you
Think of John Clare, another
Poet. He had a difficult life
With insanity building up
Like these cliffs with 320 million
Years of mud as the pre-historic
River moved in slow motion
Out of itself.

     You can claim for yourself
The salt and the water, tears
Of unchartered seas and those
Lost survivors, like yourself
Holding tight to whatever will
Not move. You can live with
The craziness of your rage
Against the waves breaking
Down your fighting spirit.

     Watch carefully how the sea works.
Relentless with its pounding heart
She comes into the bay
Of stones, rushes the wall
And backs off for breathing
Time until someone like John Clare

Or you, dying and writing poems
Stirs the waters with mud
Coming out of itself as if to escape
Once more from the asylum.
Swim, swim hard before you come
Out of yourself after all these millions
Of years. Swim from wall to wall.
You are crazy once more, in love.

SCOTTISH WATER

You move in a way that
draws those watching along
like one wave behind another.
It's the sea coming into
the gently sloped cove,
the arms of centuries old
caress and kiss. It's the mouth
of the ancient rescue at the edge
of everything being lost. Your life
steals a glance over your shoulder,
your hair much longer than before
and golden, ready to be spun by
the expert and grateful lover, one
wave gliding in, then one more.

YOU MUST HAVE YOUR FAMINE

You shout to the North Sea
From the Scottish coast.

You tear the skin from
The largest rock older

Than our talk of love
Creating all this water.

There comes a time when
You must have your

Famine, your war, domestic
Dangers. You shout

At the North Sea
And your words come back

To remind you of the storm
And that love battering

The ancient wall of warriors
Slashed into tiny pieces.

On the legs of salt
Created for you to survive

You shout at her
And she becomes the mist.

You shout, you swim until
The ice in the sea holds you still
With lust and very, very hungry.

SCOTTISH PRAYER BOOK

You've stopped for the night
And the headstrong
Dreams come in
Fighting for attention
Like the waves crashing
Against the white and black rock.
You get up quickly
To go stand
In the middle of the street.
You scream some inaudible words,
So help you God, in a prayer
For the hand around your heart,
Inside your cage of ribs,
Trying to bring you back to life.

SCRAPE

REVENGE

Never mind. The next week
Will tell the story. We can
Then find our way onto the right
Road, smother our path with oil
And white flour. You are a danger
To yourself, a gift to others.
Always giving your number
So they'll have someone to
Talk to, any time of day or night.
The sunflower is such a signal,
Like a lighthouse at the edge
Of the world. You hold on to
The stalk, the glimpse of a cloud,
Wait for the giant wave to lunge
In beautiful revenge against your stone.

WEEDS

Hers is one of those really
sad and exhausting lives.
The weeds are growing wild
and blue. There is a simple
and straightforward song,
something that explains it all.
Hers was one of those really
sad and exhausting lives.

LEARNING TO RIDE

In the second grade in Northwest Kansas in your small
     town,
You were learning to ride your bicycle. You pedaled
     along
The sidewalk gliding past large trees between you and
     the street.
You also had a "rice crispy treat" secured by unreliable
     but
Helpful teeth for the moment. It was a quiet day, most
     likely
A Sunday afternoon. You became distracted or just lost
     your
Balance both of which you have done many times since.
     Then
You hit one of those large trees straight on stopping the
     bike
But not you. You landed on the ground, sat up, pulled
     the "treat"
Out of your mouth along with some pink saliva and a
     previously
Loose tooth. You were lucky. It was 1952, your father
     was trying
To stay alive fighting a war in Korea, earning a couple
     of Bronze
Stars for bravery, while you were trading secrets with the
     "enemy,"
As your mother would say, but whom you describe to
     friends as
The cute Methodist minister's blond daughter very
     willing to share.

PUTTING DOWN

How she withstood
His care, aware
Or not. It will
Always be a question
For me. It always
Will seem more like
Treatment than care.
Or mistreatment.
Maybe a love song
Gone terribly wrong.

THE FLAPPER BIRD

There are so many ways to speak
Your heartache and give voice
To the tired and lonely blood
Flowing from the mattress out into
The hallway. The freedom fighters
Had no idea of what the
Blood would look like, so red
And life-soaked into UNESCO
Treasures. Those who survived
To tell the story do it every
Chance they get. Grease the
Gears, barely ask the question
And the bird beats the wings
Into remission, the breath
Tasting like her tongue excited
To enter the love of her life.

PHRASING

My body is not working
So good today.
Not good.
Not well.
Pick your phrase
While I go to the bathroom
Again.

HEADLINES

2016 to be year of fear
in U.S. I did not read
the article but I suppose
it could be many things:
Presidential race, Middle East,
gun violence, Planned Parenthood,
immigration, 400 families
versus the rest of us, police shootings,
the death penalty, incarceration,
so many possibilities. We don't fight
over the best poems or the worst.
Or at least that conflict never makes
Headlines. Think of that: Doty
Slips up in twelfth debate with Nye.
Primary in Iowa now leaning toward Urrea.
Nation undecided over next poetic leader.

GIVE IT YOUR ALL

I am skipping the tragic parts.
Even so there is enough
Bad news to at least give the good
A dash for the penny.

Talk into the mirror and give
It your all. But, you complain,
I did that yesterday. What?
I ask. Gave it my all, you reply.

You agree that the accumulated
Dead from centuries of war mean nothing.
I said I would skip the tragic
But then I glanced back over my shoulder.

SOMETHING TO HIDE: A SONNET

Do you have something against light?
The blinds and curtains
Are always closed
Until I open them
Sometimes not until noon.
Are you hiding something
From the world outside?
Or hiding something from

Me? Because either way
It's not working. I can
Tell when the world has
Caught on to your tricks.
As for me, I've seen your love
Between us for years in bed.

GOOD FRIDAY, AGAIN

I know I ask too many
Questions but how can
I learn and move on if
I keep silent at the back of
The room. I will cook my
Last meal myself, sneak
Into the press room to hear
Directly the latest news,
Rumors of war, the edge
Of bloodshed.

Tonight I could smell the
Out of control wildfire,
Biggest in the history of Kansas
That we know of, evacuating
Towns, burning the ranches
Within reach, the cattle clustered
Under exploding trees when they
Could have waded into the ponds
For safety. With all this news
I noticed you have the laugh
Of someone in love. I will cook my
Last meal before the betrayal.
Curious, that laugh. Mocking me
For not seeking safety in the water.

SCRAPE

As you get older
Your skin becomes
Less, not more, calloused.
Your consciously thick
Skin is disappearing
Layer by layer. You scrape
Your hand or arm
In a slight, careless
Way, and the blood
Quickly appears
Opening you to all
Possibilities of the day ahead.

CANDLE

Forty years ago
I put the car in reverse,
looked straight ahead
through the windshield
and saw the light,
a candle in her window.
I had come to say goodbye
at 3 a.m. I was crazy
in my first love and losing
the dream. In a few hours
I would be driving east,
away from the Pacific,
far away from the sea.
I don't remember what we
said. I do remember not
making love, ever, still.
I drove away, lost and weary,
longing for the bridled fear
to free the tongue, for the
courage to stay and help
her blow out the candle.
We would then watch
the smoke climb the wall,
we would never be
broken again, or fall.

DAILY PAPER

I have arranged my interior
furniture so you have a very
special place to reside in
my heart. I hope that's ok.
Let me know if that's not safe
for you. I don't want you to
feel trapped or made to take
up residence in an inappropriate
neighborhood. Trash pick up
is Thursday, daily paper tossed on porch.
Good hot water for our showers. I'll be happy
to fix anything for you.

SALT

Even the score
before the tide turns
and you find
the sunset crawling
up your back
down your front
like the hands
of water ripping
and churning in circles
sending you out
toward the vast
sweet current
tasting like fruit
you sprayed over
your body
and the salt
that preserved
you for me forever.

THE OVER-RIPE SUN

The over-ripe sun
is taking its time to find a lost sea
among all the missing
and presumed drowned bodies of
water. It is taking a step
in unknown territory
only because it is so ripe.
Otherwise it would never have the courage.
It will take a long time,
more than you care to wait.
Even if there is a good chance
it will quench your thirst,
bathe you into wholeness.

WE WANT TO BE BETTER OFF

Those you see on the screen
are the lucky ones, they
at least have some debris
to work with. Splinters of
two by fours, broken
PVC pipe, various sheets
of plywood for a roof.
Those you don't see
on the screen are the unlucky
ones. They are under the mud,
their gravesites now the foundation
for this new village. No one
wants to talk to us, standing
as we are on their buried
families. [Sorry it has been
so long in this empty search] You,
he said, are not helping with your
words, microphones, and cameras.
We want to be better off.
Find your own red mud-slide
then try being photogenic.

DEEP, LIKE AN OLD MOVIE

It will be fine.
I will sleep my deprivation
away very soon. All the craving
hangs from my arms
like apples on a tree. It all
runs deep like an old movie
about a submarine. The deeper
the more pressure on the hull, the skin
so exposed, any slight fracture
will split open causing major
damage and certain loss
on the ocean floor.

The children will make a wreath
of paper, glue and glitter
to welcome us home as heroes.
They will wait, arms aching
to lift us, their loved ones missing
at sea, a deprivation they will learn
to live with as the waves crash around them
crushing the sand into glass.

Lies I've Heard or Told

DOWN, CHILD

This is not
the usual syndrome.
The medical professionals
have tracked the heart
to a small canyon
in a small country
just below the mountains.
The down, child
apparently tries to
quiet the heart's beating
as it grieves the world's beating.

LIES I'VE HEARD OR TOLD

I love you.

I hate you.

We are now out of Iraq.

There are WMDs in Iraq so we must invade.

No, there isn't someone else.

Yes, you get the children as often as I do.

We've landed on the moon.

Algebra is easy.

I was at the library studying.

You're making this into something it's not.

You have beautiful legs.

I don't miss my dead parents.

You look twenty years younger than that.

You look ten years younger than him.

You look great!

The bottled water is better for you than tap.

I feel great!

Every joint in my body hurts.

Yes, you get the children as often as I do.

Trust me.

STAGE FOUR

A scowl of sand
forms a mask covering your
face like an ancient desert god
or a tomb. The labor of so many
works the already dangerous tiny warriors
into an army many nations
try to defeat. 'I thought maybe an ulcer,'
says one. 'I guessed it was just allergies,'
from another. Fools. They tried a wet cloth
at the bottom of the door, tape around
the windows, a lifeline from the backdoor
to the barn. Nothing worked, nothing could kill
the forecast as it metastasized into a scowl of dust.

SANDEND

On her walk to Sandend
she helped herself to the
ripening blackberries even
bringing some home in her
stained hands. The berries
were large and juicy, the stains
hard to remove. She realized
the juice had made its mark
all the way around her body,
the skin becoming its own
blackberry flesh. This only happens
on the dirt pathway to Sandend
where passion runs deep above
the sea and human life comes
so close to the sweet salt of love.

SYRIA

I speak respectfully of my broad shoulders
made fun of since I was a young girl
playing in the dusty streets near my home.

I speak of how I prefer to be cold rather
than bundled up in some bulky coat
keeping my arms bound and useless.

Did I mention how I sing with the beautiful
storms? How I love the thunder, the large
dark clouds, slashes of vibrant lightening?

But I speak mostly of my love for the rain.
And I tell my family in Damascus of these
Kansas storms, so different from my home.

When I play my violin, I am moved, not
to tears, but to exhaustion. The dread
of the distance forces the blood from my
fingers. They are grey like Aleppo and my lips.

PANSION STARI GRAD

Juliet, Juliet, that is the hurting part.
You wake up
and in the mirror
see your life
only
in black and white.
Juliet, that is the hurting part.
It's a life-threatening situation for those of you
living north of Paradise, praying in Nebraska. Juliet
open your eyes
as you wake up
see yourself
in black and white.
Your life
depends on it, north of Paradise, the hurting part.
Juliet, Juliet,
and it's grown to be
a life-threatening situation for
those of you under siege in Stari Grad, across the ocean
from Paradise, that is the hurting part,
open your eyes, see the blackbirds, thirteen
of them only in black and black
you wake up.
Your life depends
on it, the situation
threatening Paradise,
Juliet, Juliet, you are
not invited to the party, open your eyes to the life-
threatening possibilities north of Paradise.
Juliet, Juliet, that is the hurting part.

HESTER'S SITUATION

Few could see the wild child
and not think devil, demon.
Hester had a rough job, not only
to care for her little Pearl and fight
to keep her but also to carry on her breast
the "A" with golden thread skillfully
wrought with a flourish
or two or three that bravely brought eyes
to the letter (or the breasts) returning
an "up yours" to all the Boston divines.

THE FRIGATE BIRD

I look forward to Ira on NPR's Science Friday
each week. Not that I know much about science
or even remember his subjects or guests. But even
the video streaming specialist, a young woman, is so
excited about the subject of the week whether it's a
frigate bird or an almost extinct spider. They are both
so happy, it's in their voices, about the next story or the
scientist who talks about the Rover's footprints or beautiful
neon algae so deep in the sea. My spirit is lifted out of
Gaza City or Baton Rouge for a few moments, not long,
but a few childlike seconds that soon turn me back to a
world that spits out hope like the blood and teeth of
the boxer who lost.

EGYPTAIR 804

We turned hard to the left
then spun in the opposite
direction like a drunk laboring
to make up his mind. In slow
tortured motion
pieces of us fell away into space.
There went my husband and my heart
torn out of my chest
still pounding.
I stopped breathing long before we
hit the sea but I am sure I heard someone
scream about a god
as I joined the drowning dead
scratching our beautiful hieroglyphic drawings
drifting along as we did
so centuries from now professional or amateur
archeologists would attempt to translate our story, a
miraculous find, on the sandy floor of the sea.

HEAVEN

Sometimes I think that in heaven
given there is one, those of us who need it
will be allowed to finally break open the dam
and cry as much as we want, for as long
as we want. I envision it as similar to last
February 5th when I had to put down my fourteen
year old dog. He was on a stretcher on the floor
of the vet's exam room. He had been given
something to relax him, ease the pain, I put my forehead
gently on his head and had my hands under his jaw
gently on his head and had my hands under his jaw
trying to comfort him and I just sobbed and sobbed as
he died and for as long as I felt I could in front of those
few people. Heaven, perhaps, will not impose such limits.
And if you need to laugh and laugh you are welcomed.
Or maybe simply rest in silence, sleep for a hundred years.

A WORD HERE

Let's do this small
lyric together. You
think of one word:
_____. Good,
Now I will add,
"throat." Your next
word is: _____.
So, I will add, "tree."
And we will go back
and forth like that until
we make a new thing,
and we will have a gift
for each other, we will
stop fighting, everyone
will stop yelling and
shooting and dropping
cluster bombs and using
chemical weapons. We
will share this gift of
gentle words, of poetry
and peace with each
of you gathered around
the world, even just one,
especially even just one.

Five hard pieces

of rain
played their music
in concert on my gutter
tonight

        But lonely under the bridge
        spit and shake for the sake of shit
        and their music reminds the cosmic
        whisper of its significance

alone, staying away from the draining
water coming down
the hill toward the river

        pardon the world, it speaks
        for too many people serving
        as liaison
        between the evil and not so evil

and you try to figure out the difference.

CRAWL SPACE

On your own, you found a way
for days of chance
encounters with colored things that
crawled between dark rough wood
and black soft dirt, over your
legs
and into your ears. A childhood
rhyme comes to mind
or would but by now your
tongue-stuck thoughts and fears
are years
or more beyond you. Mostly people
remember you
in passing, as in passing
the stone marker, your name,
date of birth and death.

Fresh

lavender began growing
unplanted
on its own to wash the air
where the previous fragrance
was poisoned by
some hollow-hashed thoughtless hack
from a dead generation. No blame
laid. Passion back then answered
to no one. I miss you but who will know.

LIFELINE

The ink on my hand follows
the lines and wrinkles in the skin
that some call life and love. From my
fetal position on the prairie colored couch
I don't want anyone touching me, let alone
holding my hand and reading my lines like some people
divine for water or ask how I 'really' feel. No,
please, put together your own future and leave
me out of it. But not forever
although that's what it feels like. Yesterday
I held my great grandson and knowing he likes
to watch the traffic out on the street we looked out the
window with his six-month old eyes. We watched, waited.
Nothing.

HORSE AND RIDER

You have nightmares but remember
your therapist, years ago,
said the violent ones, no she *suggested*
you think the violent ones with blood
could be thought of in a positive way
as the brilliant flow of life not
the spattered, slathering of death and pain
they seemed to be. And in her office
for that few minutes of grateful insight
it worked, you could see it. Until
the next knife-involved moment of sleep
skin-mostly-red dreams coming from
somewhere and staying for a couple of days
for you to find ways to shake them loose
like a horse, tired of its rider, slams a tree.

ANOTHER WAR

You fight these internal wars
great battlefields covered with
bodies Stephen Crane couldn't
imagine. It is all so exhausting
but defense is essential not
appeasement. You are on foot now
because she stole your horse. Why not
sit down against this tree, wipe away the ants,
stop the bleeding from your wounds, wait for help.

PRAYING GLAD TELL

I pray to stop the nightmares
the ones I can't speak of except
to you the ones I can't forget
the forest enchanted old chimney's
brief and sour test of sexual skill
blood managed by money sick with fire
rancid stew of stars to slick down my hair
felony after felony touching the quiet skin
falling falling falling for the quiet skin
I'm glad, chin in hands, I can tell you all of this.

Like the ocean

the large maple sways in rhythm
with the wind, the leaves curling
and washing the rest of us with doubt
and eternal blasts of blue and red,
sky that could be the ocean and leaves
their autumn repeat of edgy calmness
and a community falling as you watch
with joyful desolation as you say those
two words aloud sitting on the ground
under the tree, hoping with the sea.

The dog (at night before bed)

I used to have to chase the _____
up to the top of _____, fence, chain link
and follow it all along the parameter
of the yard, while the _____ balanced
on the fence top. It was dark but every
night they had this ritual until the
_____ climbed up the neighbor's higher
privacy fence and ending dog's adventure
for another night-like-no-other. Last February
my dog's pain was worse than mine, much
_____, and I had to "put him down." I'd
known him longer than anyone else in my
life, 98 years or _____. People today and dogs
need each other more than ever, even with
the grief of death, wide open brown sad eyes
at the end of such a long love affair.

DECEMBER 25, 2016

Christmas music at Terminal E
            Philadelphia airport
the world is on the move
especially the children
some with cloth
            antlers, actually
many with those head ornaments
a sign of the victories achieved
                        or the pleasing of the adults

in their lives. Some moms
      have that look boarding
      the plane
that smile of endured exhaustion
like the one with a child walking
in front of her, one infant in a front sling
and one stumbling behind stepping
            on her heels. The

mom/smile is cloth, sewn in place, plastic
teeth that will break if used
                  like a glass ball
                  on the tree that falls. She is trying hard
                  to like flying home, to show she is

happy as a clasp of coal
or a diamond.

DIONYSIUS

I'm on his trail, the backwoods
of the pantheon of the light-footed
legends we live by. I need to let
the critical remarks against me
slide away like fish down a duck's back.
Didn't it rain? And what do you mean "if?"
It's always been "when!" Curl up on the couch
with your _____, enjoy a _____
and finally relax to the world or the underworld.

THE POET'S HOUSE

The moon flowers
interrupt the dark
bringing you back
from your senses
to the more familiar
bewilderment. You feel
comfortable in the imagined
thin gown and slippers
as you step so quietly
from room to room so
you can listen to
who has been tied down
to their beds for their
own good, the screaming
crazy Janes of Yeats,
the silent brooding John Clares
with almost twenty years of
slipping poems underneath
their doors. Sometimes it's
bedlam, Sylvia writing
two or three poems a day
sometimes silent as a nail
so Emily can secretly write
for years, adding them to the bundle,
to be found later, suddenly,
we all think, like a miracle.

CROSSING OVER

I can't do it by myself.
The current is so swift
and the rocks on the floor
slippery. Please take my
blue hand, it is that cold.
I am afraid of a fall
as the world begins to fall.

PROJECTION

The men in my life, _____
Hi, I'm dating so and so
from L.A. and I just wanted
you to know _____ and it
is important to keep the pattern's
in the open so I appreciate
your _____ but let's
not overlook our life
in healing others so it continues
to be a journey. Loving my life
and my own greatness so _____ you
and we may or may not
be falling in love. O, to have
a Kauai wife.

BOSNA DREAM #1

This thin soul as you may know
has nothing to do with this skin.
Nothing! Take a peek inside any Homeric
literary epic, just a glance, and it will
be clear, terribly transparent, just to
make the point. Then lift your eyes
toward the heavens and the stone-black
pillars of the adoration. That's when,
with the adoration word, you will
curl your fists into crimson, rage-filled
lovers, not hidden well enough as, contrary
to promise, they soon appear in the crosshairs.
I notice your breathing hesitate until
automatically and with a North Sea-like
crescendo you will find that voice
you've just discovered after centuries. And
everyone around will speak of the eternal search
for the Adriatic twenty-kilometer coastal claim
and whisper the public archetype of blood.

BOSNA DREAM #2

The dog next
door, named Wade,
is barking
at the leaves
scraping and crackling
against the chain-
link fence
separating the two
countries. It's a full
out wind from
the south, summer's
tornado path
but now, on this
last night of 2016,
we fly in the face
of all storms
keeping the door
locked to all
intrusion, we listen
for heat-seeking
weapons, Bosnian dogs,
hunting.

Carry on at 1 a.m.

until the, the black birds
with those red wings
of spring, cling to the
single strong stalk
in the marsh. It is a sign
of change for those of you
in love. Known for hope
spring actually sees more
suicides than the others.
I heard on the radio life
expectancy is down a tenth
of a year. So, carry on at
1 a.m. your skin-flint sparks.

HUMAN RIGHTS SABBATH-2016

Your childhood memory
is cold like an unsolved
crime, which is what the police
call a mystery remaining.
The years you've thrown
behind you come together
as a Sabbath, a rest,
a recollection on this day
of chemicals and clusters,
some choked hope in poison
dust as you collect the remains
no one you love can even hold.

SUSTAINED LAMENTATION

This is a new phrase
to me coming after a sermon
in Advent this morning.
It is December 2016, so
perhaps those two words
are a gift for this time,
this country. We are in
a national emergency and
a spiritual desperation both
leading to some of us,
some of you, anxious for a
direction or method of
sustaining lament. Remember
brokenness and wholeness are
not opposites but two sides
of the same coin, so use caution
when tossing that coin into the
air, let it drop to the ground
without inference. We could all
join the rich, be sent empty away.

COHEN'S ALLELUIA

You are trying to work your way
into a better space. Listen
to life and its songs, to death
and its whispers, to finding and
to searching: Why that punctuation
behind you? God could pound
all over this savage yard, salvage
yard and make no discoveries worth
your thin-skulled syndrome. Take
your day in mortal slathering
as an example. Dig the plow deep
into the blackened earth, hoping for some
god-shed to crawl into and your
storm-force, snow-packed face sings
the small "a" alleluia off the tongue.

BOY IN THE BOOK

The daydark is here
much sooner than expected
along with the custodial
tasks of bucket
and soap, broom and
old rag to wipe the Scottish
slate. I start at the far
end of the sacred
floor and walls and roof
and move, often on my knees,
merely removing the grime
from the toenails of clerical
misbehavior and hard sleep,
sweat curling among the hairs
of life, liberation,
libation. Last night, sitting
on the couch, watching a TV movie,
I sat alone surrounded
by the flesh and burn
of family present and loathing
and faces of abduction and
desertion, rage and smiles
just to make it the whole time
I remained on the couch
in the midst of the silence
of disbelief along with
the rag to wipe it all away.

DIVINE COMEDY

You have
a sense of humor
like the ornate
box turtle
our state
reptile. But,
I am told,
it's all in
the timing.
So,
I wait.

TIME TRAVELING

The slow station
rolled gently into view
as those departing
stood in the aisle
with coats and quiet
gladness fear and
who can tell
what else. Others
boarded with eyes
forward hoping for
a seat to themselves
because most of us
like it that way
because, well,
who can tell.

LOST AT SEA

Swales and sea gulls above
The day-dried sand that stings
Your face, while your pale skin
Flushed to pink by the cold

Dies and is gone forever except
Today. You could hold the hand
Of any lover with the same
Pale effort, indiscriminant and old.

STRANGLES

It's highly contagious
and you don't
want it. Wear the
rubber boots
and surgical
gloves when treating
the horse. The night
visions may return,
the unkind ones. Almost
deadly to your way
of thinking and your
nerve
damage. Maybe
it's the same as
removing two day old
dead lambs in utero
with a scalpel,
hope you don't
have on your hand
or near your throat
an open wound.

QUAKER MIDNIGHT

Sunday
she says
is very hard

and, yes, for
some reason, I
reply, it's been

the saddest day
of the week all
my life. Has

she heard from
her love, I ask. That's
most of the trouble,

her loneliness,
confusion. She mentions
church, that it helped

a little. I reply
but can't remember
what I said - about

church - I feel
nauseous from the
chemo. I roll over,

stop thinking about
the pain, start thinking
about the pain

around us, close my eyes
no later than ten or
around Quaker midnight.

Try carrying the other's

burden for just
a short time. You
can see the light
of strict kindness
like a hit and run
accident sending
the victim into the air
fighting for life,
touching the stars
and sweeping the
highway with
the long arms
of singular strife.
Carry the other's burden
like a hit and run
fighting for life,
the long arms
touching the stars
of singular strife
like a hit and run
fighting for life.

THE GOSPEL GOODS

There was no snow today
And it didn't even rhyme.
You forced semi-articulate words
From your vocal appetite in time

For local residents to hear
The loud, street-corner sermon fake
A word-of-god praise from horse-
Induced ecstasy and you will take

The final devil, cleanse it
From me as the grit and grime
Of nights driveling in lost houses
Burns and burns from Jesus' crime.

There was

rain today,
the kind of slow soaking
dark rain that makes a break
with the light of day
allowing the ground to drink
and eyes to open gently
to the horizon and black earth.
Graveyards across the high prairie
surrounded by barbed wire
find consolation on days like this.

THE TRAINS

It's about the same as
every night. The trains
moving north through
the bedroom window
and out the bathroom
with a much smaller window.
I've tried since I was a kid
to figure out how that happened
but this is a magic land
with love and loss, seventy year
marriages, then a massive stroke,
hospice and in two short weeks' time
a burial on the prairie.
So much magic. Just ask one of the
train conductors or anyone
traveling the yellow brick road.

The nightlight

throws shadows against the wall
like an abuser,
like a slob dishing it out
against his only son.
The nightlight is placed in your room
to give you comfort, but you know
it's true, not-so-clandestine, purpose.

FALL TO WINTER

I thought of your hand
reaching across the café table
touching my arm so kindly.
Do you remember the sky
we watched? The strong clouds
and the birds flying into the fearful
unknown, escaping one season
for another? They moved
using careful instinct, with a connection
I still, I still wish for us
to escape one season for another.

THE CAIRN

The heart coiled and died
like a hot red pepper
dried up and discarded in the garden.
Don't touch me, it said, I am not ready.
The birds came only so close because they understood.
Gradually, other dead things gathered around
the heart as they were discarded
and dried up as well. 'O my god,
I'm crawling out of my skin,' was over-heard
from under the cairn. The gathering grew. The day
faded into dark, our brothers and sisters
came to the memorial for the dried up and discarded.
It has since been used as a marker for our path
into the dreams, centuries ahead, toxic playing fields
seen through thought-dead shadows cast by the moon
shining on the pile of coiled hearts and dry.

THE QUARRY

The abandoned quarry was our
community swimming pool. It had
just enough water from rain and runoff
for us to wade out in our underwear
and swim but still be able to touch the bottom
with our feet. It was, as you would expect,
a test of bravery among the several boys
choosing to disobey our parents' warning. On hot
summer days we would walk through the Maine woods
to the water-filled rock quarry, strip-down and splash into
our own private pool. I was the youngest therefore
also a target for the oldest one. As I stood ankle-deep in the
water he came up behind me, put one hand on the back of
my neck and the other down my underpants. As he felt around,
my feet sunk deeper into the shallow mud. I was stuck and
would see myself as the youngest for the rest of my life.
When he finished, I sat down in the water, balancing
myself with my two hands. My right hand immediately
became numb and pulling it into the air, I saw a deep cut
from broken glass just below the surface. The blood mixed
with the mud and the water. Tonight I see that scar as I
write, write this poem. Every night I write poems
to try to heal the scars but so often I just tear off the scab.

PLEASURE

'Keep awake,' I kept telling myself
All night. The street was too quiet,
Maybe it was the rain. Or the chill
In the air. No one telling some casual
Lie to leave the apartment. No one so
Lonely that it's not even worth the
Simplest of pleasures. Here comes a car
Moving slowly, first one in an hour.
It closes in on the curb, I take a
Step, barely out of the shadows.
"You pervert," he yells and throws a
Beer bottle at me. It breaks on the sidewalk
Behind me. The car speeds away and I quickly
Move back against the abandoned building.
The dark is sucking the life out of me instead
Of the other way around. It is still raining.
I'm shaking a little more and it's not the air.

GRASSROOTS

I spent the afternoon making calls
for the Democratic Party in my Kansas
county. Mostly to older patriots
using Advance Voting ballots, making
sure, they had received their ballots from
the county clerk. I'm very fearful of
"massive voter fraud." Isn't everyone?
A lot of people weren't home on Saturday
so, I left many recorded messages. I had a
long conversation with Ora, age 91.
"I've seen a lot of elections and this
is the craziest one of all." I agreed
and asked her if she had more
questions of me. Ora said, "No,
but I've got a lot of questions for the idiot
Republicans, like our governor." She
went on, Ora at 91. "My mother-in-law,
she's dead now so I can say this, was
such a blind-headed Republican that she'd
vote for a retarded snail if it was her party."
I ignored her politically incorrect language,
she's 91, we're in Kansas, and she's a Democrat.

LEARNING TO SPEAK

You've been crying a lot recently
at the sparrows and cardinals feeding
on the other side of the large window
in the kitchen. The clouds disturb
whatever happiness your life started with
in the morning. "A warm human plumpness
settled down on his brain" (Joyce's *Ulysses*).
There's the sentence that tells us all how
you feel having to wait out the oral decay
of aphasia and the hard work of recovery.
You're crying a lot, phoneme, by word, by god.

Tomorrow is a tight fit

although another poet wrote
it would be a "tight fist." For you
the truth belongs
against the black boulders like fat soldiers
in a children's story or rhyme.
They are never as simple as our
simple desires make them with ghosts,
lions and two or three syllable words
at the most. When you or I pay attention
as we watch the rock-bashing sea
we will also watch the children's difficult days
then our own dawn emerges tight as a fit can get.

THE LIGHTENING LAB

Was it murder? Or simply
a push at the top of the stairs
soul's hands clapping
breathing stopped
without the breaking of the neck
negatively charged attracted to the
positive and here in the lab
for lightening before and after a normal
lunch and we all are normal for the sake
of all experiments left for us in this lifetime.

THE CLEAN FIELD

After being harvested and harrowed
your neighbor's sheep and goats wander
the clean field. The rain falling
now will soon cause the loose
grains to sprout and the stock
will graze slowly, almost like
statues or toys from far away
along the fence line next to the sea.
Then the rocks you see like gray
steel beams angled and thrusting
seismic power from the gravel, sand
and seaweed. Gazing toward Arctic
waters you must watch as you
stumble, tremble with the thought
that the same Arctic still sends air
to you cold enough for your haunted
bones to empty their marrow-life deep
and forever to be ice-bound and waiting.

IT'S A HARD LIFE

In 1670 the harbor was begun,
finished fourteen years later, first
on the Morayshire coast. You walk near
the sea wall in your stubborn
stone-hacked way. The loves you carried
on your scrubbed shoulders betray
the salt lips of the drowned and those
who ran to the inland forest of the
fishwives, flesh wives, early to die.

WRITING IN SCOTLAND

The sea from the north rises
in a storm-rush against the ancient madness
of rock and sin. Daylight of the morning
frightened by the deadly dive of birds
bright that day of all the years
loved and dissolved, using the "f" word
in graceful conversations to end
all intercourse. At least spell the words
correctly and give us a clear view
as you stretch your arm around her shoulders,
those smooth olive-touched, that unable-to-describe
body of work labeled and labored into your life.

CROSSING THE IRISH SEA

"The way up
and the way down
are one." --Heraclitus

This is one of those

turboprop

planes with the wing above

the fuselage so you feel

like you are hanging by a thread –

shades of Jonathan Edwards and the angry God –

above the sea

and if you sin, SNAP,

you fall

something like 19,000 feet

all drowned out

before you hit

the water. But this flight is pure,

without sin, quiet, for the moment

until the clouds

reflecting the wet morning light

hide from sight

the runway.

THE COST OF IT ALL

The feel of this carved swimmer
making small waves keeps the heart
beating and gives my breath a catch
like a fish. You wade through
the inch-deep, fleece-like water
meeting you where the shore allows
the sea to touch your toes and other
places you won't let me near. I'm mad
at her because she's mad at me. She says
it's done. You go your own direction,
it's the way of love in your eyes.
Salted, you awaken to the grace you paid for.

LOVE IN SCOTLAND EVEN IF

it is a fake day.
Here in Scotland, we no longer
Talk constantly
About salmon or rain.
You may notice, if you visit,
That we are deeper
Than you've come
To understand.
We say thank you to the driver
As we get off the bus.
You want to go to Cullen?
I'll drive you. And even if
It is a fake day, with laundry
Drying on the line in ten minutes,
Waves only inches high so they
Can't be described as "breaking,"
I'll get your coffee and read
The news aloud to you from
Any paper we can buy.
Here in Scotland, in my family,
It's more than the waves that "break."

2 POEMS IN BODY OF EMAIL

The flesh plucked roughly away
Told the father and son finding
The two poems in the shallows
That the body had been dead

For some time. No identification
Found with either of them and no
Family to make final arrangements.
The sacred words came from a stranger.

YOUR TRAINING DOES NOT

Your training does not
Explain the way you wear
Your hair, smile or not.
And you know that mom
Has lived long enough now
To be a problem. And the plane
We took to fly to Ireland
Was the same type that crashed
Monday in Indonesia.
The evidence keeps piling up
And you refuse to stand
As a witness to your own
Ego, the self-centered, controlling
Painkiller that saves both of us
From the everyday curse we breathe.

U.S. SUBMARINE VETERANS
MEMORIAL HIGHWAY

Huck and Jim
Missed the Ohio River.
Was it the fog?
Or the strong current?
Was it Samuel Clemens
Or Mark Twain?
We find life in the strangest
Places
And death.
And how often
We are blind to the fork
In the river. Keep your feet
In your own damn stream,
Let the catfish
Skim the bottom mud
To survive.

THE LIGHT

The light
　　how it makes
a lover swim
　　　the breaststroke

as opposed to
　　the backstroke
or rejection
　　　by another name.

PHRASE

You watch the ice
Begin its life on the
Skeletal trees.
There is a glaze of fear
Building across your face
Stretching like a second skin
And the hospice light glows
From the barn to the county road.
Your body is not working
So well today.
Not too good
Or not too well?
"Pick the suitable phrase,"
You say, "while I use the bathroom
Again."
While you are away
The visitor, from a nearby cattle ranch,
Puffs up your pillow,
Gets you a fresh glass of water and new straw.
You return, notice the kindness,
And exchange a thank you
For the visitor's you're welcome.
You reach for the simple words
That express -- goodbye, and,
I've lived a full life.

YOUR STORY

Every story has a flip side
And a life so ingenious
That another could sweep
It away after it dies
On the sidewalk, unidentified.

A life so ingenious that another
Could sweep it away, turn
The flip side away from sight
So she could go to the city park,
She was feeling so much better.

FROZEN

-Translated by anonymous

I.

I'm a world unto myself.

Just like you

And you and all of us gathered here

At the edge of the forest

Of ice. Songs miraculously

Remembered by generations

Of the loved, the un, the lost

And the one I saw melted

The other day.

II.

Your hand is gentle along its path

On my leg. This honeymoon has begun

Long before the word was ever invented.

Now, there are so many of us to watch over,

Each angel needing two or three to carry on.

AS I GROW OLDER

I want fifteen (for now) important items
tended to in a timely manner:

Trim my toenails
Trim my fingernails
Trim nose and ear hairs.
Make sure my socks are clean
And my underwear, especially my underwear
And my glasses
I want my hair cut handsomely short and neat
    like my scotch
I want my children, grandchildren and
    great grandchildren to know I
    am alive until I am not
Find the damn democrats some GUTS
Somewhere
Ask Cora to explain "SELF AS SOULMATE"
Treat every faith and non-faith
    Community carefully, we are
    all terribly wounded
I am a "veteran of the cross" so see
    if some money can come of it
When I stop laughing
    Someone pick up where I left off
Do you have any questions?

WHY THE WILL TO PUNISH?

YOU FORGIVE, IN THEORY

THE FRONT LINE

Boulevar, Mostar, Bosnia and Herzegovina 2020

Today I met a lifetime goal.
I was walking behind an old man,
Perhaps five or ten years younger
Than me. We were practicing
Good social distancing because
Of the COVID-19 pandemic as if
Some paramilitary 20-year old
Had shouted us into the direction
Of a death camp. We were walking
Slowly because, this time, no one was
Rushing us along the Boulevar, the front
Line in the 1990's wars, new buildings
Shined in the sunlight like those advertisements
For vacations in Dubai. Then the tall
Bombed out Sniper's Tower standing watch
Over it all. I watched him as he so
Skillfully clasped his hands behind
His back as he walked, as he thought.
I realized that I had been waiting – not
Consciously – to get to that age where I
Could put my own hands together
Behind my back, lean a little forward,
Walk along the front line, dignified,
Wise, pondering the future or the past,
Wise and tired as a Bosnian old man.

SPACIAL PREPOSITIONS

Mostar, BiH siege, 1993 – 1994

What is beautiful
when there is
no world?

Do only fools
walk in
the cold?

The trumpet
is dead so why
are you moving?

Only the crows
come for a coffee,
and the sadly

Sad. Now they will
die to whom
they write

a sentence. Why
the will
to punish?

FERAL

--Front line, Mostar, 1993

I just found out that the brain
Uses up calories. You all knew
That, right, having paid attention
In biology class? I knew some things
And enjoyed the dissection of
The frog more than most. But I am
Now distracted by the lace curtains
In my study and the feral pink sky

As the sun sets, as usual, in the west.
I lose track of my job, at this window,
Here on the front line, the boulevard
Below, as a sniper looking for movement.
I am a lousy soldier and pay
For it. They called it a flesh wound.

SOAP

Sometimes it's the ancient
ordinary things that
gets the stink blowed
off you. If it's a lively
breeze then you hope it is
from the north. It's the best
for scouring words like that one
from the skin with some guarantee
of a day or two clean. But
when you go to the south wind,
the Slavic twist from Blagai
to your town, it brings the dust
and plastic bags flittering
like bats and then you glow
like the desert in the late sun
and face more need for sorcery
instead of scoury words. And
in the event of an unusual crosswind
bounding off the rocks of the mountains
surrounding your city, you are going
to be forced back to the ancient remedy.

THE MEDIUM HOTEL

A normal human life is all
you want. You can't find
it here in the midst of
family and lost books
you never wanted to read
anyway. You light another
cigarette, your fifth in
six minutes. You claim
you have lost seven years
of your life. You tell me
you are religious so why
has all this happened, you ask?

Anyplace but here will help.
No more medium, screwed up
people in your life. You
will find another hotel where
they appreciate your work, –
leaving good tips, no gentle
words of thanks, and no one
falls in love with you.

MARE ON MY CHEST

I don't know sometimes where
to find the hope when friends
die and nephews take themselves
out. Anger is just another
loss. The clouds wish they
could dump all that rain
and move on. The earth is
desperate for rescue although
the chances are as good as in
Vegas. The skin I imagine
is just that. Outside, along
the Neretva some dog, a new one,
barks and sets off some car
alarm we should all pay attention to.
Anger is just another loss.

NOTE FOUND IN THE NERETVA

just like my frig
but I don't have
any magnets
from America
you will have to send
me a package
but with magnets and
all kinds of magic things
and some postcards in it
and so much love
just arrived home
from work
how are you

INHUMATION

The hardest part
is breaking the ground.

This is not the bog
of peat that would

preserve the human
into sometimes even

clearer recognition. This
is hard pan breaking

the shovels forcing us
to curse the ground

but even then it is
nothing but the lazy

lace of bones anywhere
they might land

and the scattering of
shoes, underwear, of family

resemblance, leaving only
a wide space for the jaw.

AGITA

You are Italian-Bosnian
with anxiety and stress –
normal – but how do you
tell me what you are feeling?
What do you care about most now?

Our life is like a bone on bone
knee, no mediating cartilage to
stop the scraping, save our love.

PERILS OF POMEGRANITES

The bone chill of morning concentration
brings a quiet across the meadow Bosniak
broken by the last of the underage girls raped
by daddy generals as upstanding citizens of our
beautiful city and the mountains beyond. If you
have the stomach to read a few lines of allegations
or witness testimony which ice the blood, read on, and on

BOSNIAN CATENATIVE VERBS

Thousands of miles, face to face
During that day
In the museum in Travnik
You taste the
Bitter air, the lips of so much striving,
The tongue struggling to make
A grammar of love like the paintings
Of Monet, one lily pond hundreds
Of times, close enough
For an illegal touch. The ambiguous gossip
Of color with verbs brushed
Into each other like our love
Was an accident of one
Infinitive after another, infinite
Across an ocean with syntax
Like 'I love that man,' poetic
Catenatives that live thousands
Of miles, face to face.

BAILIWICK

Above a whisper
or below a whisper
what will you find?
A place of safety
or one of fear?

Don't ask me so many
questions, am I the one
under suspicion?

You may go but be
warned that the raven
is watching you. You
could be sent back
to the old country
anytime. I watch
the birds carefully,
all kinds of birds,
not because I am afraid

but the opposite.
The wings and the
flight give me hope.
What about you
tasting that orange,

do you know how

mean we can all be

above or below

that Balkan whisper?

the whole bright town sighs

BEYOND THAT

He wore his time
on his wrist, a circle
of blue. Beyond that
his hope
for a lasting
kindness born
of the toughness
of life. He learned
about being kind
when he felt
on his own skin
the lack of it.

SUPERHERO

across the sky and late adolescence
the last trick from the bag
is lost, somewhere you misplaced it
and you are in front of everyone. they
watch your dark eyes as if you
are the horror show. you could scare
all of them to death if you felt the
power over them they know you
have. but these perverse hormones
only frighten you, leave you standing
naked. there is no strength of will
as you hope for a superhero to swoop
down and save you from the laughter
and take you away from all that is
peripheral, emulated, or cross-legged.

COGNITIVE FLEXIBILITY

In theory, you dream a dragon
Spreading its wings with the anxiety
Of anyone trying to avoid St. George
Or another, front-of-the-cave,
Near-death, experience.

Wave upon wave to crush
The bones of daily beasts and reality-
Based plot lines trolling the waters
Of the loch where the mist hangs
Right over the stain of the disappeared.

It has grown to be an epidemic
As we all look over our shoulders
While others watch ahead, alert to find us
To keep us quiet forever. It is almost a matter
Of faith, of careful breathing, as we fall.

Infinity is a natural wonder, more egregious
And circumspect than any flight of birds
Making its way to a southern continent now
Drifting alone in a lonely sea where it can only
Be discovered like Neptune, by numerical prediction.

You dream again about the dragon
But now you are the one spreading your wings
Tough as an ancient angel. Your voice makes
Silent the meadows and mountains pounding the
Earth for mercy. It is finished, you forgive, in theory.

AGORAPHOBIA

You just want to close your eyes to the world.
Instead, you'll just stay within the walls,
prison-like, of this house. And smoke. And drink
coffee. The neighbor will bring the mail and paper
to your door. What happened in your childhood
to make you cringe at the thought of shopping, going
out to dinner with friends? You watch morning
T.V., the afternoon soaps for some drama. And
the news. The news. That's it. You glance outside.

REFUGEE

My whole system is geared
For the good old days, hour
After hour of removing life
Support while the faithful
Wife organizes grief sessions
For the kids and embracing
The doctor and nurses, thanking
Them for all we have done,
Says we feel like family
And please stay in touch
For old times sake. A few
Drinks later she will
Volunteer for the inner circle
Of an Italian drama based
On Dante. She will flesh out
All the unfortunate refugees
Making it this far but having
Everything against them, they
Stumbled back into the sea.

The Theremin

you waited until they died
then you officially buried them
all. why? you had some
secret grudge against wailing?
you didn't like early electric
music? just caress the air with
your hands and you have music,
eerie, something very strange but
delicious. maybe the metal antennas
reminded you of some childhood
incident. but you did not get
them all, sorry to tell you.
official or not, some escaped
and are waiting for your visit.
wave your hands your delicate way,
let the theremin weep and wail.

THE WEATHER (forecast/foreplay)

I am barely a woman at all.
Have you seen how small I am?
Of course not, never in all these
layers of pink, brown and red.
Not to mention this large umbrella
that would cover my entire naked
body. I bought it because of
the weather forecast I saw this
morning. I turned it on as I
was dressing to come here. The woman
had bare arms, a tan and was good
at forecasting. I tried to imitate her
movements, the way she seemed to
caress the magic map even though
I know she did not actually come near
touching even one of those countries.
But I liked her tactics, wanted to feel
the touch I wanted to feel in my life.
And you can be sure, as I tap your knee
when we talk that I am playing with the weather
forecast, with you, with us as you watch me slowly
twirl this new umbrella I bought today because
of the forecasting lady. Maybe, it will rain
and I will need to decide whether or not
to share this new, large umbrella with you.

THE CROFTER

It's the muddling around
in the croft with the blue and blighted door
that gives you the reputation
up one street, down another
until it crawls and sweeps with its long
flesh-punched tail finally
back into the secret lake
and the whole bright town sighs its globed relief.

RUN FACING TRAFFIC

Time to go,
I can just
sense it.
Not fear,
as I realized
today. Because
I have survived.
Carefully, look
straight into the
headlights, carry
the burden
of your race,
the foot steps
behind you,
the hard breathing
but even, like the
stride, a healthy
heart, the movement
of air, never give anyone
a free shot, always,
always run facing the traffic.

PENCIL

Coloring the page
I am told to stay
Within the lines,
This color or
That one for the
Eyes or the tail.

But the creature on
The page before
My eyes is wanting
A color of its own.
Cries out for
A sharp pencil.

To grasp in it's fist to
Tear through the paper
One corner to the
Other, across the
Page, creating a
Crumbled, forbidden life.

A FLIGHT TO SOMEWHERE

I have forgotten those times
others call memorable. My
most intimate mysteries,
simply not knowing when to stop --
lovely, slight, hurtful
and up to my waste
in the swirling sea looking like
a calendar photo. I simply
didn't know when to stop.

"Go t' sleep ya' little baby"

It's as simple a beginning as this
and as difficult. What will come next?
A walk along the sea two hundred miles
from Norway? The glowing green night sky
stuns your nerves, a lucid reminder
of the little we know as the bedtime
rituals with our children bring our sea-bones
aching up to the surface, are carried by
the tides towards the islands as a gift
wrapped in salt, faltering with each step.
Please, all ye babies, the harp blesses your sleep.

EARTHQUAKES IN KANSAS

Here are my mom and dad on a good day:
That was before the earthquakes began
And they stopped standing for photographs,
Stopped standing near each other. They each
Had their individual press conferences with
Rage and erotic dimensions but mostly
Martial law, clever, self-assured until
She left and he drove off the road on a
Dark turn, the red car filled with ecstasy,
His body flying from Tecate toward Yuma.

GAZA SONNET #1

Having bombed the children,

homes, hospitals,

used phosphorus

on the playgrounds

pieces bouncing onto

the skin of six-year old's

it burns and keeps

burning its way *(scream here!)*

through to the bone.

It's a long way to the sea.

It's a long way to the sea.

It's a long way to the sea.

It's a long way to the sea.

It's a long way, my children.

WHEAT

Here are some of those things:
Gradually the system begins
to break down with ransom
and capture. Soon the snow, as we
will see, never measures up to
expectations. Here in south central,
the meadowlark sits on the remaining
brick foundation bringing her particular
ballad to Vermont Street. And the wheat
being in the ground, red winter
can begin. It took four days after removing
life support. Red winter has begun.

Physical Education

LETTER

Hi, I am fine, thanks
for asking. For the first
time I had therapy
two days in a row. It was
helpful but also brought
up a lot of crap
and questions. I believe
I was sexually abused
by my 5th grade teacher
during a summer when he
brought me and another male
classmate to his summer
cottage at Cape Cod. I can't
remember specifics,
hardly any details
but my gut passes on
secret information to me.

The week at the Cape
was supposed to be an honor
as only two boys were selected –
each summer. Anyway, today
I am not doing so great,
with the leftover taste of
salt water in my mouth.

GARDEN

If it blooms
it's a flower.
You never weed
the garden
because it is all
unknown and
beautiful. Besides,
what have those
wild plants
done to you?

MOTHER, MAY I?

You tell everyone you are well
but not about
the hauntings. You notice
the relief on their faces
that they have asked you
as promised, not
that you are well.
That you are well
is not of concern,
not, as promised. Why do
they say the light is blinding?
The "suspicious" brushfire in L.A.
is growing. The morgue at al Shifa
is filled with strips of anonymous flesh
and splintered bones of the children.
You tell everyone you are well
but not about
the hauntings you notice.

IRIS

There is a message
in that word.
For real. And you
can discover the

truth by caution
and straight talk
before the marriage,
look – the purple and white.

TANGLE EYE

We all keep
Working on what
It means
To be human.
That is the summary.
Some win prizes,
Get interviews on NPR.
You have kept looking
Straight ahead
All your life
With one eye
Staring at the sun,
The other tangled
In hope
For what it means.

A HISTORY OF OKLAHOMA

We have the best
documented life with you
having been conceived
in the Upper Volta
or maybe the southern flow
of the Neosho. It's a
matter of record no one
wrote down. Fortunate
for you no photographs
remain. Memory tells you there is only
last year, then Jesus,
the Renaissance, then
of course, you are limited
in your rage to dirt roads,
one continent
and a father exploring
the unknown, previously
taught as flat,
world.

PONY, MONTANA

1.

The bridge, made of large concrete squares, held
   for the moment.

2.

She told me there was suffocation in the room.

3.

It is all one-sided, you always pouring yourself into
   the cup.

4.

She laid on the floor for two days, her right leg
   paralyzed, saying, "It's not mine."

5.

In Spanish, if a negative follows a verb, a negative
   must precede the verb, it's the rule.

6.

There is that urge again, to run away to open ground.

7.

She said that the sky was raining but only horse tears.

8.

The Girl Scouts' pumpkin carving is still on.

9.

In kindergarten I was the one in show & tell with a
    time limit.

10.

Dismal seems like a brighter word than desolation.

BLIND OUTLET

No one wants to be around anymore.
I just don't have any vivid memories
recognizing a halt or sublime
performance some idea like the
invasion of the beauty spring in the languaging
of the mouth and languishing
when we can. Circe is popular now
and may be around the corner, around
the bed, hanging out. She might
want to be with you with her own visiting
memories. Welcome traveler. My promise
if you sleep with me is survival
and a permanent shadow.

PHOTO FROM SCOTLAND #2

Today
the sea   is full

of white horses. Far out the blue
is calm
like the music
of the harp

with breath   in and breath   out.
Simple. And is my
rage the same? I talk to some friend
or stranger then the   familiar
desire

comes
to him or to her
in the face with my already
automatically
clenched fist and/but I make love

to the white horses
full of the sea.

DUBLIN AIRPORT

Magdalena is called for her flight
to Brussels. We all follow her
onto the bus taking us to the connecting
plane. It is an ecstatic time for everyone.
The temperature has dropped to 7 Celsius.
Celtic is in the air as a Jet Blue plane
takes off into the dark morning sky.
Jesus, she says to me. I say, don't touch
me, yet. We'll all meet later – in Brussels –
Magdalena, me, the disciples. Then Judas
whispered in my ear to save embarrassment.
Sir, this is not your flight. You have been
enchanted by a false heart. Remember, stay
away from love, then you won't risk betrayal.

AVINE FUNERAL

it's a variant form
of avian to be used
in mortified ways
to change the living
wing-work of the flames
of birds all around
this house and the sea,
variant love-making
the darkness dash against
the last trees left
in this lush landscape
and from Heaven escape
to invert evil to live
dashing night to diamonds.

THE RIGHT TO BE FORGOTTEN: A SONNET

The sea birds are a morning chorus,
restive in their wakefulness. Soon
the same lonely coastal music
will bring the restless
waves to the point of breaking and invoke
the "right to be forgotten."
In these countries, under the force
of legal power you or someone you love

can be forgotten, it is the legal
right to be deleted. So often there have been
those times when you have wanted
to just disappear, never to be seen again
or remembered like so many soldiers or children
invading an unknown beach, dragged out to sea.

SOUTHWEST FL. 36

Ok, babe,
we need you,
Paul Wright,
if you're still
going to Little Rock
we are here, babe,
Gate 20, the door
is still open.
Or, babe, listen,
you could join some
of these soldiers
and go to Ft. Campbell
although you might need
basic, training I mean,
you could go to Syria
with the elites, babe,
figure it out, I'm
closing the door, honey,
I need you.

EIGHTH GRADE

I was the kid who hid
in the arts
and crafts closet
in eighth grade. It was
fear. It was dance time
for Physical Education
which terrified me.
Dancing and being educated
physically.

MAYBE A RIB

It was funeral food.
Everyone sat at round
tables, heads down as
they chewed and swallowed,
swallowed and coughed.
Eight people could sit
at each table though
each table was overflowing.

I watched as people moved
their lips as if talking
to the next person. No sound
collided with any other
sound to create completed
words. Eyes were barely
open like the tears, barely.

The young girls chose the wrong
house for a sleep over. Rage
was the language choking
on the tongue. It was
funeral food. A few guests
went back for seconds, more
lime jello, coffee, or a rib.

ELISIONS

The light is in the center
of the ceiling. You will return
because soon friends will be dying
and you will be asked
to officiate the funeral
or visit them in their sickness,
say comforting words, try
to get them to smile.
It will be an act of breaking away
or of joining together, something,
in either case, of eternal omission.

THE CORRUPTION OF ADVENT

O, how shall I receive thee
Rend the heavens wild
Light the lamp of the Baptists cry?
Soon we'll all be near ye.

Bring the gifts of gold and myrrh
Twisted star, broken heart
Expect the father's child to leap
Soon to birth the angel's word.

FRESH FISH SOLD HERE #1

It's an old joke
like fumbleheed
but I can't remember it
so
I should ask
the person who told me.

Go down, go down.
I can't find
the person
with information
about this old joke
because she is in the states
and I am in Bosnia
and Herzegovina,
perhaps you know?

Or
maybe Faulkner
could devise a machine
to find gold
and jokes or some other
mystery in the cotton
lynching and here we start

to get serious. You can't run,
you can't jog, get out of a car

without risking your life
to the fumbleheed, not
a joke. Go down, Moses.
Go down, *mmmmmm*
mazing.

IMPEDIMENT

His head hurts
thinking about having
to put words
in his mouth.
So much the enemy.

The snatching away
of syllables by electrified
muscle tissue
shoots of pain rooting
everywhere from brain

to legs. He has to think
about every phoneme
hours ahead of time. He needs
some space, not someone
jumping in to "help"

which it doesn't. He gets angry
when you can't just wait
for his inside sparks
to catch up to the larynx
tongue. And then the blood

on the tongue, the repetition
of sound, the same damn
sound. Always the same sound

as something cramming words
up his throat

against the will.
So much the enemy.
Against the brain and pediment
into sharp pain blood
pooling around the white teeth.

AN OLDER MAN

Fifty years later, following some death,
I arranged for the fate
of my next fire. I consciously oppressed
my soul's cousin
and was told I could now only sing solo.

I AM USING SATIRE, OR NOT

GLEMM BULK FOOD GOSPEL BOOKSTORE

Does this mean the food
Is bulky, awkward to handle,
Impossible to grip with two hands or four
Or you can buy it by the case
Or pallet-load to put in the back
Of the truck until three months
Is up and you return
To stock up on provisions?
Unlike a monograph this writing
Is on multiple subjects like horses,
Windows, empty stomachs, bad news,
Good news, land of the lost, land of the
Brave, cowardice, open doors, rain,
Ice, books, food, no food, water, no
Water, music, cacophony, green,
Soil, seeds, frustration,
Defeat, victory, frustration (again), buttress,
Voice, no voice, rage, laughter, hope
Humor. Preach this list then comeback
To me. I will load your pickup, don't bother
About the tip you never bothered with
In the first place. Vocabulary cards will help
Your total education. It will help you hold
Your fist high in the air, o my children,
Give away the bulk food, the books, the good
News as is only fair and true, bulky with hope.

INFLECTION POINT

A frog on my window
Is swept off
By the windshield wiper.
I drive down the street
In the humidity of
This tropical brain fog.

The war is long over
But my lungs
I gave to the blue
Soldier near the river
Crawling toward me
Pleading for a deep breath.

We are all having
Strange and violent nightmares
Since August. It has been
Documented. Suicides? Yes.
Domestic violence? Yes.
The blood streaks across the windshield.

TOWARD THE BITTER LAKES

The water is kind to me today
carrying me as if affectionate
to a new edge of the wild.

In the foreseeable future which
is returning in the old naïve
way as if affectionate to the edge.

With the intuition of a stroke or an
earthquake, she took my hand as if
with kind intention leading me to the lake.

conditional logic

low pressure moving
across the region
is expected

so I am wary
of you risking
it all. you say his way
of thinking is
fascinating,
so is covid-19, the spikes

to bring an unsettled day.

a swarm of bees

for George Floyd

it's only a video sent
by a friend. her father's
bees embracing a branch
and the trunk of a tree
moving barely enough
to notice. in fact, the first
thing is the sound. a
grinding, slow business
cooking above your head,
without hurry, no place
to go without your mama,
so the charge is stinging
without intent to kill.

Introducing

on behalf of the others,
those who couldn't be,
for whatever reason
just couldn't,
be. But in their absence
let me acknowledge
the courage of the saints
not with us, the holiest
of fathers who will never
say their goodbye's not
because they are dead
but from simple lying
completely to the end.
May they return in peace
to face the sons and daughters,
to face the children who have
truly died right before their eyes.

POPE CANCELS EASTER FOR PUBLIC

Easter, 2020

This is Italy, spring, 2020.
It's hard to explain to you
exactly what fear! I'm being
wrapped up in a cocoon of anther
from the flame or the flower
burning as we speak of deep
yearning for touch and freedom,
hands waving in the air, the gloss
in the sky with a dangerous
proximity. With Easter canceled
for the public, we are on our own
to find some loose hope floating,
just buoyant in the air. Since we
are the public we should unify
and find the Easter evidently

taking place even though not for
us. We can be creative. We can
be alert. When you discover some
light, stumble across options
in some field, let the rest of us know.
Shout it out. Hope cannot be canceled
even for the least of these, or the last.

SEVENTH SYMPHONY

Can you hear the flute
Maybe in the last movement
Like heaven although better
Because I don't know what
Heaven is like, not really,
Not at all. But I can hear
And see the flute in Leningrad,
The city of Lenin. Slavic. Frozen
In the siege. Then the strings dance
For the dead wrapped in sheets
Lying on sleds to be taken away.
The muted trumpets carry
Their tune across the mountain
West, the great desert, more
Mountains and then the sea
To shatter the glass towers
Built for other tragedies
And heroes. A friend asked,
Do they serve bourbon in
Heaven? Again, I know nothing
About heaven. Why, all at once,
Are people asking me about religion?
And why, all of a sudden, are TV news
Reporters showing so much anger
Toward elected officials and saying
To their colleagues, please stay safe, I love you?

PASSION FRUIT

The sky breaks open
on this Palm
Sunday-Passion Sunday-
the passion of my work
from the tree like fruit
too ripe for the hungers
of this world. But here
come the children
allowed their moment
of entry, carrying the palms
singing joyful "Alleluias"
for Jesus in greeting and
hopeful smiles. Forgive them
for they don´t know. Forgive
them for they don´t know
what is next. They cannot
hear the others singing,
"Hosanna," save us.

EASTER

Grief is familiar with all of us,
So full of possession and a sense
Of global warning. To be ravished
By the already cursed brings a
Medieval tone to this life and
So we watch the fortress gates
Carefully. No one in, no one out.
Carefully, the firing of the twenty-
One gun salute echoes west along
The rocks of the Scottish coast
Toward the Highlands where some
People have escaped for centuries
But usually not successfully. Hear
The philosophical lecture on the attempts
To escape from danger to hoped for
Safety. It is only philosophical and
The lecture ends early like a movie
Fade away into the dark. Remember,
With me you can never know
If I am using satire, or not.

WILDERNESS

The Snake River
into the Tetons
feeding this lake
big and cold,
I am told,
like your heart.

A MOMENT IN TIME

I wish someone
had a photograph.
Any photograph.
It is still a mystery
to me just how a
moment in time
and space can be
captured and made
to be still. Can
someone, anyone, help
me figure this out?
It doesn't feel right --
like Margaret Hayes
taking her last breath
right in front of me.

SHE DOESN'T LIKE WATER

You can cut all the flowers but you can't keep spring from coming.
-Neruda

Anything to drink but water. She hates it.
Maybe something from childhood
or a lost full moon or one of her children
strayed into traffic. But she only shows
strength and resilience in the worst of days
and nights of which she is so familiar. She would
even ask why people will ask if this poem is about
me. Do all poets really write about themselves?
Why can't this one be written in the third
person and mean it? People really do have
deep issues from childhood basements or
elementary teachers and their summer cottages.
She never could remember a wife being around. Soon
we all stray into the traffic and that word can
have many meanings like in the movie where
traffic means drugs, death, sadness, and ends
with a kid's baseball game on a dirt field
in Tijuana. Who forced her to drink water
when it was only pain for her? Does this poet
really mean water when that word is used? What
happened to her childhood? My bet is on the lost full moon.

re-forestation with stutter

watch the ferns in their
dense forni-
cation. don't be squeamish
like your br-
other or watch
too closely as
i did. father will be him-
self and push you ah-
way when you come
up to him
to say, I-
'm sorry.

ANCIENT TEXT (1)

A fragment

Gilgamish woke-up calling
For his mother in the midst
Of lusty dreams and omens.
"Mom! Like a Hittite of heaven
He fell on me, too heavy
For me." He had fear down around
His ankles, and felt a solitary
Childhood with ragged edges
And dogs betraying even their
Owners in the middle of the streets
And they all became his likeness.
Then "I loved him like a woman,"
Which is where the mother of
Gilgamish really started listening.

Michael Poage was born in Virginia. He has published fifteen books of poetry, most recently, *WHY THE WILL TO PUNISH?*, Spartan Press, 2023. He served as the Poet-in-Residence at Dzemal Bijedic University in Mostar, Bosnia & Herzegovina, 2018, and has taught English literature and ESL courses in Latvia and, virtually, in Thailand as well as in Bosnia and Herzegovina. He lives in Wichita, Kansas with his wife, the historian, teacher, and activist, Dr. Gretchen Eick.

This project was made possible, in part, by generous support from the Osage Arts Community.

Osage Arts Community provides temporary time, space and support for the creation of new artistic works in a retreat format, serving creative people of all kinds — visual artists, composers, poets, fiction and nonfiction writers. Located on a 152-acre farm in an isolated rural mountainside setting in Central Missouri and bordered by ¾ of a mile of the Gasconade River, OAC provides residencies to those working alone, as well as welcoming collaborative teams, offering living space and workspace in a country environment to emerging and mid-career artists. For more information, visit us at www.osageac.org

Osage Arts Community